MA RAINEY

and the classic blues singers

DERRICK STEWART-BAXTER

STEIN AND DAY / *Publishers* / New York

First published, in both hard cover and paperback editions, in the United States of America by Stein and Day / *Publishers* / 1970.

Printed in England
Stein and Day / *Publishers* / 7 East 48 Street, New York, N.Y. 10017
SBN 8128-1317-0 (hard cover)
    8128-1321-9 (paperback)

Produced by November Books Limited
Designed by Ian Cameron
House editor: Elizabeth Kingsley-Rowe

This book is dedicated with love and affection to one of the great Blues Queens, Victoria Spivey, who by her help made this book possible. Also to my great friend John Van Praagh who first gave me the taste for the Classic Blues.

Photographs
By the author: 27, 31, 71 right, 100, 101
From the author's collection: 103; Lucille Hegamin 14, 21; Edith Wilson, 29; Rosa Henderson 33
Paul Oliver's collection: 10 (right), 24, 39, 41, 45, 46, 50, 52, 65, 77, 80, 82, 84, 95, 97, 99
Riverside Records (photographer Donald Silverstein): 57
Victoria Spivey: 63, 71 (left), 89, 96
Printed ephemera from the collections of Paul Oliver and the author

MA RAINEY

series edited by Paul Oliver

Contents

Towards a Definition

One of the pitfalls of jazz and blues criticism is that most critics, in an effort to simplify understanding of the subject, try desperately hard to classify the music by placing it in tight little pigeon holes. Now, this is all very well, but music, unfortunately, like all the arts, refuses to conform. There is continuous change; various styles and fashions merge and fade until something fresh appears. It follows, therefore, that the moment one has caged the bird, it finds a crack in the pigeon hole and flies away. Over the last decade the blues have suffered very considerably from over-classification; writers have traced the Mississippi Delta singers' influences, the Texas blues pianists' characteristics, the rural and urban styles (even down to those of specific cities like Chicago and Detroit) with very mixed success. With the best of intentions, they have confused rather than enlightened. Is it any wonder, then, that the Classic Blues story can be likened to an unfinished jig-saw puzzle with several pieces missing, or not fitting into the complete picture? Perhaps it is just as well for our sanity that this form of singing is now only a dim memory to most of us although occasionally echoes from the past can be heard from a few surviving artists. If the researchers had turned to the Classic period of blues singing by the women, who knows what fresh confusion would have resulted?

As it is, the position is complex enough and it would seem that few critics or collectors have more than a vague idea as to what constitutes Classic Blues. The definition we have may be ambiguous, but it cannot be ignored. Over the years it has become more and more meaningless; for example, nearly every woman singer seems to have been put into this category, from the rawest country moaners to the more sophisticated performers: a completely ridiculous situation. Let us see if we can arrive at something more satisfactory.

As the great Classic period has faded into limbo, and is not likely to be revived in the forseeable future, the task of classification should not be beyond us. Of all the inappropriate labels ever tagged on to the blues, Classic must surely take first prize. A glance at my dictionary gives the following explanation: ' . . . a student of the ancient classics; a standard work, writers of the first rank, or their works' (*Chambers' English Dictionary*). Even if this is applied to music, it is difficult to see how any of the female singers fit the description. The women performers of the 'twenties and early 'thirties had many virtues, but their style – or styles – were hybrid, and contained elements other than pure blues. It would have been more acceptable had it been applied to such bluesmen as Blind Lemon Jefferson, Charlie Patton, Bukka White, Skip James, Robert Johnson, or even a 'songster' such as Mississippi John Hurt; but this was not the case, the term was used exclusively for the women.

At first the word Classic referred to such Titans as Ma Rainey, Bessie Smith, Clara Smith (no relation), Bertha 'Chippie' Hill, Sippie Wallace, Lucille Hegamin, Rosa Henderson, and, of course, Victoria Spivey. There may have been others, but these were the so-called trend setters. As time went by, and more and more records were issued by more and more artists – good, bad and indifferent – the term was extended until it became valueless as a means of identification. If we take the eight I have named as a guide, we will see that all of them, regardless of their actual style, had two things in common: their comparatively wide range of material, including other songs than blues, and the debt they owed to the tent shows and the vaudeville stage. George Melly writing in The Observer Colour Supplement (July 27th, 1969) gave a much needed boost to these neglected ladies and made the point that 'At their best the "classic" blues represent that fragile but precious moment in developing art form when feeling and technique are in perfect accord, and in Bessie Smith the times provided the necessary genius to give this moment concrete expression.'

It is sad that, with rare exceptions, writers and critics have chosen to ignore these singers; a few lines here and there on Ma Rainey, Ida Cox and Bessie Smith, is just about the sum total over the last ten years. As they sing ballads and vaudeville songs and are, more often than not, accompanied by jazz musicians, they are condemned without trial. This is a ludicrous situation. It is, I believe, the vaudeville influence which is the drawback, and both purist and modernist will ignore the very idea of a music-hall based vocalist. Yet it should be realised that these women were performing for their own people: it was for the black public they were singing. As Melly says: 'There is (in the songs) a certain amount of unkind satire at the expense of the naive country Negro and especially the religious-minded, but it was contained within a racial context. In the vaudeville blues there is a proportion of the worthless, the mechanical, the contrived, but there is also a gaiety, a vitality, a sense of good time'. In short, the classic blues singer was a stage performer who came up with the glorious music hall tradition. That is why the work of such fine singers as Bessie Tucker and Elzadie Robinson and their contemporaries in style does not fall into the category of Classic Blues as I define them.

The young enthusiast is hardly aware – and if he is, he ignores the fact – that it was a woman who recorded the first blues, and it is true to say that without her the great male singers, the real roots of the blues, would never have been recorded, and the story of the blues as we know them would never have been written or re-searched. We owe a debt of gratitude to Mamie Smith, the pioneer. Yet how often do we see her name mentioned in magazines devoted to the subject? Alas, the young critics pour scorn on the head of anyone who does not conform to their narrow outlook and limited ideas.

As Paul Oliver has pointed out in his book *The Story of the Blues* (Barrie & Rockliff, The Cresset Press, London, and Chilton Books, Philadelphia, 1969), the blues are a state of mind. Furthermore, they are music which expresses this condition. The blues reflect the cry of the forgotten man and woman, the shout for freedom, the boast of the virile man, the wrath of the frustrated, and the ironical chuckle of the fatalist; but this is not all: they also reflect the agony of insecurity, the poverty and the hunger of the workless, the despair of the bereaved and the cryptic humour of the cynic.

But let there be no mistake, the blues are also a social music. Today, they are of paramount importance as an entertainment. They are the ideal music for the enjoyment of drinking and dancing, and, at the other extreme, they are the songs of a certain segregated class – the American Negro – for in them he can find an outlet for his problems. Thus, the blues can be a music of creative artists within the folk community. It makes little difference whether it be in the deep rural South, or in the teeming ghettos of Chicago and Detroit. Blues are all things to all men of the race; they are the songs of the primitive guitarist sitting beside the railroad track; they are, too, the sound of some barrel-house pianist pounding away far into the Mississippi night; they are the commercial Rock of the blues bands; they are the earthy ribald 'dozens' of the

Right: As late as 1924 the Paramount catalogue listed no country blues singers at all. Blues guitarists and blues pianists were also absent, but such 'Classic' blues women as Ida Cox, Lucille Hegamin, Rose (sic) Henderson and Mme. 'Ma' Rainey were all listed.

medicine show, or the cabaret blues of the edge-of-town club; they are certainly contained in the show-biz routines of the travelling troupes, and in the latest hit of the recording star, or an unknown field worker singing as he toils. The tale has been distorted over the years, and we have never known the full truth. It cannot be complete without a survey of the Classic Blues era, and that is what this book is about.

The Classic Blues - Vaudeville Style

It is one of life's small ironies that Mamie Smith, the most historically important of all black singers, was an artist of only moderate ability. If we are to base our judgement on her recorded work, and that is all we have left on which to form an opinion, we find that her voice lacked the richness of the truly great women artists who were to follow her into the recording studios in the years to come. Seldom was she really involved in what she was singing, and at times she lapsed into the sentimental; this can be heard in both her lyrics and the melody of certain numbers. There may appear to be an outward toughness, but occasionally the marshmallow at the roots comes to the surface. *What Have I Done To Make You Feel This Way* is an example. Nevertheless, her place in blues history cannot be denied; it was her pioneering work that paved the way for every other blues artist, regardless of style.

Mamie Smith was born in Cincinnati, Ohio, in 1883; a pretty child who was to grow up into a strikingly handsome woman.

Left: Mamie Smith; Right: Perry Bradford.

There was never any doubt that she would become a professional singer, and from an early age she had an ardent ambition to become a stage star. When quite young she was a member of a white act known as the Four Dancing Mitchells, and this, as far as we know, was her first professional job. The Mitchells worked in and around the state and the youngster gained valuable experience from this team. She then took a step upward, joining the celebrated Salem Tutt Whitney Show, The Smart Set. As this management was famous in its day, it was a good springboard from which to launch a career, and by the time she was twenty-nine, in 1913, she had arrived at Harlem. It was not long before she found herself in demand, with plenty of work to keep her financially solvent, if not exactly rich. She could be found singing in the numerous Harlem Cabarets whose names, to the jazz lover, have a familiar ring. She sang at Barron Wilkins', Leroy's, Edmund's, Percy Brown's and the Gold Grabins, and of course in the Negro theatres. It was hard, unceasing work, but show business makes heavy demands on those who embrace it. To take the plunge into such a world is one of the greatest of all gambles, and luck inevitably plays almost as big a part as talent.

It was in 1920 that she met the man who was to play the biggest part in her colourful life, the composer, band leader and singer, Perry Bradford. At that time, young Bradford, a dynamic entertainer, had a burning ambition which smouldered beneath the surface of his rather extrovert exterior. His one great desire was to see the music of his people recognised and appreciated. He knew from his experience in travelling minstrel shows all over America, that the white people loved to hear his songs and the blues of his race. In his book, *Born With The Blues* (Oak Publications), he claimed that American whites would 'go slumming' into Negro areas, to the theatres and clubs to hear and appreciate, if not entirely understand, the music. Thus he was determined to badger the recording moguls until he achieved success. He was convinced that, if he could get a big recording company really interested, he could prove his point and that success would follow automatically. In Mamie Smith he felt he had the very person to perform his dressed up blues songs. With incredible energy, and the ability never to take no for an answer, Bradford haunted the various studios, pestered the executives, and finally talked himself and Mamie into the OKeh studios, a feat bordering on the miraculous. To persuade the hard-headed recording men to listen to – let alone to record – a completely unknown black girl singing

11

in a strange idiom was an achievement without parallel in the popular music world. Full credit should also be given to Fred Hager, recording manager for OKeh Records, for having the foresight to give Miss Smith her chance. In his otherwise very bitter book, Bradford pays a just tribute to Mr Hager. He writes: 'I must right here, however, give credit where credit is due. The number one man in the successful operation was Mr Hager, the recording manager for the OKeh Company. It was he taking a chance, and I mean *taking a chance* with his position (when all other companies had turned me down) to issue on record a Negro girl.'

It was on February 14th, 1920, that the first recording ever made by a black blues singer took place and history was made. Mamie sang two compositions by Perry Bradford, *That Thing Called Love* and *You Can't Keep A Good Man Down*. When the disc was issued, the sales were most gratifying, and in August of the same year she was back at OKeh; it was then that the real breakthrough came. Nobody could have foreseen the sensation that was to occur. Mamie, accompanied by a small band with Willie the Lion Smith on piano, sang two more Bradford blues, *Crazy Blues* and *It's Right Here For You*. In the early 'twenties when song plugging and television had not become the brain-washing persuaders that there are today, the disc was virtually a sales block buster. In the first month of issue *Crazy Blues* sold 75,000 copies at a dollar each, and continued to be highly successful for many months. It was one of the first big hits for the young OKeh company. Hearing the song after all these years, it is hard to understand what all the fuss was about. It is an unambitious little blues which Bradford wrote in 1912 and which he originally called *Nervous Blues*. It remained unpublished until 1915, when Perry changed the title to *Crazy Blues*. The melodic line is easy to absorb and Mamie, being a good professional, puts it across adequately enough. Her performance, the simplicity of the lyrics and uncomplicated tune, must have helped bring success, and perhaps the time was ripe for change. Certainly the Negroes supported Mamie Smith and were proud of her success. The backing *It's Right Here For You* is a much better song, but it was *Crazy Blues* that hit the target.

Reading Bradford's book and the various letters he was to write until his death, it is obvious that he was a very embittered man with a large chip on his shoulder, and his attitude made him some enemies. Throughout the years there have been attempts to

OKeh

4113-A

Contralto
With
Rega Orchestra

THAT THING CALLED LOVE

(Perry Bradford)

MAMIE SMITH

GENERAL PHONOGRAPH CORPORATION NEW YORK

minimise the part he played in Mamie's debut. Even Willie the Lion Smith in his fine book *Music On My Mind* pays him less than his due. He states that on the *Crazy Blues* date he cannot recall him being in the studio. Be that as it may, it cannot then be denied that Mr Bradford worked untiringly to promote both Mamie Smith and his own compositions. Perry is one of a legion of Negro musicians who have experienced a raw deal from the music business, and it is no wonder that from time to time the victims hit back, and hatred and bitterness creep into their public statements.

After these highly successful sessions, Mamie Smith was an established star and for the next decade toured the country appearing at all the best nightclubs and theatres. Nor did she neglect her recording career, recording nearly a hundred songs in seven years. The musicians she used were always top class: Coleman Hawkins, Johnny Dunn, Buster Bailey, Bubber Miley

13

Above: Mamie Smith in 1920 with a band similar to the one which made Crazy Blues. *It included Ernest 'Sticky' Elliott (clarinet), Dope Andrews (trombone), Addington Major (trumpet), Leroy Parker (violin) and Willie the Lion Smith on piano.*

and Garvin Bushell all appeared with her during this period. Her last studio date was on February 19th, 1931, when she cut five titles for OKeh: *Don't Advertise Your Man, Golfing Papa, Jenny's Ball, Keep A Song In Your Soul* and a re-make of *Don't Advertise Your Man.* For many years *Jenny's Ball* was the only one issued in Britain and it is one of her best, with a fine accompanying band which included Bill Dillard and Ward Pinkett on trumpets and Jimmy Archey on trombone. It is rumoured that during her career she received over 100,000 dollars in royalties. She lived in style with a home in New York City and another in Jamaica, Long Island. She spared herself nothing: fancy cars, expensive furnishings and a procession of lovers filled her life. Her escapades and temperamental outbursts were food for the gossip columnists. Alas, it could not last; the Wall Street Crash of 1929 and the resultant Depression hit the music business extremely hard, and blues singers in particular. The enforced retirement was tragic for these ladies, and other employment had to be found. Mamie's success and big spending while she had the money was legendary, but this was over, and Mamie, like so many others, waited on the sidelines for prosperity to return; but it never happened. In 1940, at the age of forty-seven, she made an effort to stage a comeback, and she was featured in a number of short films. The most interesting was 'Paradise in Harlem' in which the famous song writer, Sidney Easton, co-starred. In this picture she re-created her biggest success, *Crazy Blues*, under a fresh title, *Harlem Blues*. In spite of up-dated lyrics and the aid of Lucky Millinder's Orchestra, the picture failed to produce work for Mamie Smith, and with her health failing and her fortune gone, she found herself nearly penniless. Len Kunstadt, in a moving tribute to her in the magazine 'Record Research' wrote: 'The generation who had made her "Queen" were either gone or had forgotten her. On September 16th, 1946 at the age of 63 years, 3 months and 21

The Chicago Defender for March 23, 1929 announced Mamie Smith's 'debut in talking pictures'. Eleven years later she made a number of one- and two-reelers. Right: at the height of her fame.

Adelaide Hall.

He will be booked for six weeks, playing the Public theaters, for the William Morris office before sailing.

"THE BLUES SINGER"

Mamie Smith, the queen of the blues, will soon make her debut in talking pictures in 'The Blues Singer,' a title that we all know is well within the keeping of this great blues singer.

Mamie Smith, the first of our Race to become popular as a recording artist, also opened the way for others of the Race to become exclusive record artists.

She will have a cast of 200 natural voices and the actual filming and synchronizing of 'The Blues Singer' begins the first of April.

WRITING STARS

Eddie Cantor surprised the profession a few months ago when he

days, after a two year illness in residence at the Harlem Hospital in New York City, Mamie Smith passed away. She was buried in a mass grave with no stone and no identification in the Frederick Douglas Memorial Park in Staten Island, New York. Except for a 3 × 5 card in the Memorial Park's Office files, Mamie could have completely disappeared off the side of the earth.'

An effort was made to have a monument and a private grave made for her. I have no idea if the private grave has been made, but as yet the monument has failed to arrive. Let Victoria Spivey, the great Classic Blues singer, have the last word, for she heard her in person, many times. It would appear that she was much better in the flesh than on record. Said Victoria: 'The City Auditorium (in Houston, Texas) was jammed with at least 3,500 people and for the first time in my life I saw the Blues Queen; I'm speaking about the early 'twenties, and I DID see something! Miss Smith walked on that stage and I could not breathe for a minute. She threw those big sparkling eyes on us with that lovely smile showing those pearly teeth with a diamond the size of one of her teeth. Then I looked at her dress. Nothing but sequins and rhinestones, plus a velvet cape with fur on it. We all went wild. And then she sang – she tore the house apart. Between numbers while the band was playing she would make a complete change in about a minute, and was back in record time for her next selection. Her full voice filled the entire auditorium without the use of mikes like we use today. That was singing the blues! I was really inspired and kept plugging to become a singer.' So the pioneer passed on, remembered by a few, but forgotten by most.

The Classic Blues singers worked in shows, cabarets, road shows, barnstorming their way across the country. They appeared on stages, in theatres, both good and bad, in films, and any work that came their way they took. They did this until they retired with the decline of the idiom. The life of a singer of this kind can be summarised by a detailed study of one representative artist. What can be said about her can be applied to all of them to a varying degree. They all played the same circuits, all had similar experiences which sometimes affected their music. They lived, they laughed, they cried, and above all, they travelled! The story of Lucille Hegamin is a good example.

In November 1920, a petite, sweet-voiced vaudeville artist with a liking for blues and blues ballads recorded for the Arto label *The Jazz Me Blues* and *Everbody's Blues*, and thus Lucille Hegamin became the second Classic Blues lady to be immortalised or

Lucille Hegamin about 1917. In spite of her demure appearance she was an exciting singer at the De Luxe Cafe and Elite No. 2.

shellac. The disc was a big success, subsequently being issued on eight different labels (including the celebrated Black Swan). The month previously, with Fletcher Henderson on piano, she cut a test pressing for Victor, but the company for some unaccountable reason never called Miss Hegamin back, and so lost a very lucrative addition to their roster.

Lucille's clear, rich voice, with its perfect diction, and its jazz feeling, was well in the vaudeville tradition, and her repertoire was wide. With all the music-hall overtones, she was still an extremely good singer of jazz-based blues, and, like Mamie Smith, achieved great fame during her career.

Lucille Nelson, to use her maiden name, was born in Macon, Georgia in the early part of the century; the family consisted of three sisters and one brother, none of whom were musically inclined, at least not to the extent of taking it up professionally. 'I can't remember when I began to sing in church and the local theatres, but I do know that I was very young. It was before the words jazz and blues came to be used. I was what they call a natural singer, anyway, I had no formal training, just picked it up as I went along. Of course, I sang nearly all the popular ballads and ragtime tunes of the day, anything that took my fancy, we all did,' Miss Hegamin told me when I met her in New York.

At fifteen she joined one of the early Leonard Harper stock companies. Harper had a shrewd ear for musical talent, and saw in this young girl a future star. One of the first songs she ever sang was an unknown piece she had picked up from somebody, called *Piano Man*. Lucille smiled and said, 'Not the one later recorded by Earl Hines and featuring his piano, this one was different'. Eventually the company ran out of money in Peoria, Illinois, and no-one was paid. 'So I left pretty quick and made for Chicago, which was not far away. That seems a long time ago, mind you it was. 1914 was the year – and a lot has happened since then!'

Chicago proved to be a lucky town for Lucille and, for the next four years she was climbing ever upward and becoming known to an eager public needing entertainment. She was billed as the Georgia Peach and was singing in all the clubs around town. 'Oh, I played all the popular spots, including Bill Zewis' Mineral Café, that was on 35th and State. Dan Parrish provided the piano accompaniment there. I was also singing at Charlie Letts, on 31st and State, and at the Sherman Blackwell, 34th and State. My pianist was my husband, Bill Hegamin, and believe me, he was one of the greatest, and I don't say this because he was my man!'

She also worked at the Elite No. 2, 3445 South State Street. A publicity handout at that time describes it as 'A palatial café – a mecca for high class amusement (known for) best grades Chinese and American foods – the interior the most beautiful and perfectly appointed of any café and Buffet of the race in the country – the musical entertainment will be the best in the city'. Certainly the music must have been wonderful, for starring with Miss Hegamin was the famous Tony Jackson, the composer of *Pretty Baby*, as well as such fine singers as Elvira Johnson and Caroline Williams. The song and dance man was William Crump. However, it was Jackson who impressed Lucille the most. 'That man was tremendous, he had a new song for us nearly every night. I'd rather sing with Tony than any other player. If you sang twenty-five choruses, Jackson would be there with twenty-five different improvisations. It is so sad that he never got the recognition he deserved before he died. Everyone in the world must know his *Pretty Baby*, yet who has heard of Tony Jackson? Do you know, I was the very first one to sing that song of his?' During her Chicago days, Lucille appeared at another celebrated café, the De Luxe, and here Jelly Roll Morton was the house pianist with Ollie Powers as drummer-vocalist. 'Yes, Jelly worked with me at the De Luxe the first time he came to Chicago, and that was when he wrote *Jelly Roll Blues*; I have the original manuscript he gave me.'

It is interesting to read some of the press advertisements which Len Kunstadt has in his files; from the 'Chicago Defender' March 6th, 1915, comes this gem: 'Miss Bessie La Belle at the De Luxe, Sunday night – phenomenal baritone singer – Miss La Belle will be assisted by Mr Ollie Powers, tenor singer and Miss Lucille Hegabon (sic) soprano. A staff of newspaper reporters have engaged a table for this evening.'

Those four years in Chicago were good ones and she remembers them vividly: 'I was a cabaret artist in those days, and never had to play theatres, and I sang everything from blues to popular songs, in a jazz style. I think I can say without bragging that I made the *St Louis Blues* popular in Chicago; this was one of my feature numbers. I am proud to say that in those early days I worked with all the best artists. It had to end sometime, and when my husband went out to the West Coast, I, of course, went with him.'

She arrived in Los Angeles about the middle of 1918 and had no trouble in finding work, for her Chicago reputation had preceded her. At Hite's Cabaret situated on 4th and Central, the pianist was a New Zealander called Ollie Prince Bell. Bill Hegamin was featured with his band at Bill Brown's Café, and Lucille also sang with his orchestra. It was a fine group, which included such good musicians as Paul Howard and John Spikes in the reed section. It was in Los Angeles that she acquired another tag name. 'The Blues Singer Supreme', and her star was still rising. 'I became very good friends with the Spikes brothers and at this time Jelly Roll was writing one of his most famous tunes *Mama Nita*, it's all part of history now, and I never realised I was playing a role in it. I'll give you an example of what I mean: at this time I was singing such wonderful blues songs as *Beale Street* and *Tishomingo*, those were becoming very popular and I had to sing them, but I was not aware that they would live as long as they have.'

1919 came and New York was opening its doors to musicians, cabaret artists and blues singers. It was time to move on, a time to conquer fresh territories. So the Hegamins packed their belongings and came to that most fascinating of all places, that cruel bitch of a city that can fly one to stardom, or with one swift, lethal blow bring one crashing to earth. The fickle jade looked kindly on Lucille, she embraced her and gave her a welcome she will never forget. New York is like that, a metropolis of many moods, a melting pot of all that is good and bad, in short a mecca only for those who have courage and ability, but above all, ability.

Singers and musicians were everywhere, and work for those with talent was not hard to find. Into this world of musical activity came Lucille, but she was prepared; after all, young as she might be, she had a wealth of experience behind her. Added to all this, her success in both Chicago and the West Coast had not passed unnoticed. Her story at this point is not unlike that of any other young artist trying to make a name. A round of night clubs and cabarets, most of which have faded into the past. The list of those in which she sang is almost endless, but it is the Libia club that Lucille remembers with particular affection, for it was there that her recording career started. Lucille seemed to walk right back into the long distant past as she related her story. 'A guy by the name of Albury who came from Baltimore was looking for me. He eventually found me working at this Libia club, he certainly knew his way around and got to the right people and that's how I got my break. Albury was part composer of *Everybody's Blues*, but he wasn't really a musician. The band was organised by my husband, who was on piano, it was a pickup group and the sax player Clarence Harris used them fairly regularly; Kaiser Marshall was the drummer, James Revey played trombone and Bob Escudero was on tuba. It was like starting all over again, for I felt that I was not all that well known in New York, not like on the West Coast. The real turning point was when I sang at Happy Rhone's All Star Show.

MANHATTAN CASINO.
APRIL 22nd, 1921

PROGRAMME

Broadway Jimmie
In Songs
Late of **"See Saw Co."**

Miss Lucille Hegamin
"The Chicago Cyclone"
Courtesy of the
Arto Phonograph Co.

Farrell & Hatch
Singing Their Latest Song Success
" I LIKE YOU"
Assisted by
Mr. Wilbur White

Mr. James P. Johnson

Courtesy of the

Q. R. S. Piano Rolls Co.

Assisted by His Four Piano Fiends

Happy Rhone's All Star Show played the Manhattan Casino (left) with Lucille Hegamin (right) getting star billing.

I can still remember that date, April 30th, 1920. I made quite an impression, and was soon asked back for two more Rhone shows, and these were really big things. They were huge events in Harlem with everyone waiting to hear them. I tell you, you really had to wail for there were no mikes. It's much easier today, but then you just *had* to have a voice – there was no faking'.

Happy Rhone's Carnival Midnight Cabaret was always an all-star concert with a huge orchestra, perhaps bigger than was really necessary, but Rhone believed in doing everything that way – this was how he made his shows so popular. The customers never felt they were cheated, so it was a good showcase for any artist.

That February Lucille's record was in all the music shops, and it soon began to sell extremely well. So in May of that year Lucille Hegamin, backed by full publicity from Arto, took to the road for a long tour of the country, playing all through Pennsylvania, West Virginia and Ohio. It was about this time that she made up the name for her accompanying band. She called them The Blue Flame Syncopators; it included Charlie Irvis on trombone, Bill Hegamin on piano and Harvey Boone on alto sax. When recording, she added some members of the Sam Wooding Orchestra.

June 1921 saw the issue of another big hit, *Arkansas Blues*, which had been recorded the previous February. The sales soared in a few weeks and continued to improve for many months. It was a smash hit and her reputation throughout America increased. Like her first recording, this, too, was issued on several labels and various companies were rapidly buying up the masters of her discs so that they could cash in on her success.

It is inevitable that an account of the life story of such artists is inclined to get blurred at the edges and, if the writer is not careful, the saga can deteriorate into a list of names of people with whom they have worked. These ladies of the blues and vaudeville stage were thorough professionals and their services were much in demand; Mamie Smith and Lucille Hegamin were the pioneers and their contribution to jazz and blues was very considerable. In fact they anticipated the jazz blues style of such singers as Jimmy Rushing, Joe Turner and Jimmy Witherspoon by many years. It is important, therefore, to trace their careers in some detail.

November 1921 saw Miss Hegamin back in New York City as a feature artist at the Shuffle Inn on 131st and 7th Avenue and here she sang a very popular hit song of the period, *All By Myself* and, of course, *Arkansas Blues*. The pit band at this club contained some fine musicians: Herb Fleming on trombone and Bill Hegamin on piano being the most notable.

1921 and 1922 were booming years for popular music and a glance at what was happening in New York makes interesting reading. Productions came in a constant stream: Lew Leslie's Plantation Revue, with the unforgetable Florence Mills; Liza, with Gertrude Saunders as its star; Plantation Days, with the superb Sam Wooding Orchestra in the pit; and Strut Miss Lizzie, with the well loved Bert Williams, were just a few of the marvellous shows that could be seen.

Early in 1922, at a dance held in the Manhattan Casino, one of the attractions was a blues singing contest. Taking part were such famous singers as Trixie Smith, Daisy Martin, Alice Carter and Lucille Hegamin. Nobel Sissle was the Master of Ceremonies, and the judges included Major Fiorello La Guardia, later to become mayor of the city. The winner of the contest was Trixie Smith, but Lucille came a very close second with her *Arkansas Blues* song.

Her work at the Shuffle Inn and her extremely good performance at the blues contest brought her a starring role in the now famous revue, Shuffle Along. At its peak, this production was so popular that two companies were on the road, both with top class artists. Lucille was in the second of these. It should be emphasised that this was in no way a second-rate company, but a genuine facsimile of the original Broadway production. Miss Hegamin played the part which Florence Mills was performing at the 63rd Street Theatre. She relates: 'There was little time to learn the show, and to make matters worse all my baggage disappeared. We opened in Wilkesbarre, Pennsylvania, with me not knowing what was what. However, after three of four days' tension wondering where my wardrobe had gone, it turned up, and from then on, I was Okay.' It was a hard schedule, and from February to May they played one-nighters, but the show, with its big reputation, did magnificent business, so all the hard work was worthwhile. Two of Lucille's feature numbers were *Gipsy Blues* and *I'm Craving For That Kind of Love*, which, unfortunately, she never recorded. The end came with startling suddenness: 'We were playing the Montauk Theatre in Brooklyn' said Lucille, 'it was a week's run, but when we arrived at the theatre one evening we found the closing notices on the board. We were stunned. I never knew quite what happened, but it was over some disagreement with the No. 1 company. To make it worse we had a full house on the evening before we closed!'

Her recording contract with Arto ended just about the time she joined Shuffle Along, but this did not worry her unduly as she was able to record some dates with both Paramount and a label called Plaza. She told Leonard Kunstadt: 'Mr Collins, the road manager for our Shuffle Along show, made arrangements a few times to hold the train at least three minutes in order for me to get to New York and back to make the records. All this would happen on a Saturday night in order for me to get to New York on Sunday to record. Sunday was the only day I had free from the show. I remember having Sam Wooding's band on one of my dates at this time.' This must have been just after the show had folded, on July 16th, 1922, when she cut two titles with Wooding's orchestra, *I've Got To Cool My Puppies* and *Send Back My*

Lucille Hegamin—the south's favorite— cyclonic exponent of dark town melodies.

624	Hard Hearted Hannah—Vocal	Lucille Hegamin
	Easy Goin' Mama—Vocal	Lucille Hegamin
494	Chattanooga Man—Vocal Blues	Lucille Hegamin
	Rampart St. Blues—Vocal Blues	Lucille Hegamin
450	Always Be Careful Mamma—Vocal Blues	Lucille Hegamin
	Reckless Daddy—Vocal Blues	Lucille Hegamin
433	Saint Louis Gal—Vocal Blues	Lucille Hegamin
	Sam Jones Blues—Vocal Blues	Lucille Hegamin

Honey Man.

'Actually', said Lucille, 'the closing of Shuffle Along did not hurt me at all. The next week I was featured at the Lafayette Theatre. Soon after this date I got an idea for my own show. I contacted a very fine singer and dancer, "Broadway" Jimmy Parker, who had just finished a show on Broadway, and at the same time I met Cyril Fullerton, who was to become my pianist in later years. He was at Howard University, but he had left to lead a group of jazzmen I needed for my show, Jazz Jubilee. The personnel, so far as I can remember, was Deamus Deans, trumpet, a guy by the name of Wilson, trombone, I've forgotten his first name, Harold Hatter, on sax, and George Barbour on drums. Of course Cyril Fullerton was on piano. That's how it started out, but there were some changes and additions later on. This act ran for about twenty or thirty minutes, featuring me extensively, and we were lucky enough to get on the influential Loew's circuit. My act was a very fast one, and I had three costume changes in the short time I was on. Broadway Jimmy featured his famous routine which he called The George Walker Strut. I sang some of my recording successes and these went down very well. I can assure you it was a hard act for anyone to follow, and I think there were a lot of complaints lodged with the front office by other artists. It was a pretty rugged time! I remember that once we doubled by opening at the Loew's State in Boston, Mass., and then rushing over to the Loew's Orpheum in the same city. Some time later we picked up the wonderful Johnny Dunn; he could really wail the blues. Johnny was *the* blues accompanist and every trumpeter tried to copy his style. We made a feature spot for him playing his own arrangement of *St James' Infirmary*. Johnny was so much in demand that he only stayed with us for a few months, we were all sorry to see him leave. Another great musician we added to our band was Don Redman. We also picked up a good banjoist, Sterling Conway, who played with Duke Ellington for a time.'

While her act was on the road, she was approached by Frank Hennings of Cameo records, and in a very short time she was signed as an exclusive Cameo artist. 'This was good, for I was allowed to pick the band I wanted to accompany me. I got the best musicians I could and searched everywhere for them. I got some from Will Vodery's Plantation Review band. I also used Don Redman and Sterling Conway. I nearly had Johnny Dunn on one of these sessions, but at the last moment he had to cry off. That man just had too much work.'

Lucille was now becoming a very big star, and for some four years she recorded for the Cameo company. In this period she cut over forty sides. It was she who made *Aggravatin' Papa* such a hit (it is still being recorded to this day). She also recorded such fine blues as *Rampart Street Blues*, *Land of Cotton Blues*, *Bleeding Hearted Blues* and *Down Hearted Blues*. It was with her *He May Be Your Man, But He Comes To See Me Sometimes* that she will always be remembered. It was her greatest success, and although pianist Lemuel Fowler composed the song, it is with Lucille Hegamin that it will always be associated. She recorded it many times for many labels, and other stars have featured it, among them Lizzie Miles. It is one of those blues songs that lives on long after the composer and the singers are forgotten. Without doubt she was one of Cameo's brightest stars, but it worked both ways, for in a short time Lucille was being billed as 'The Cameo Girl'.

The autumn of 1923 found her in a musical comedy, Creole Follies, which toured the country. In December of the same year, with Cyril Fullerton as her accompanist, she went solo on the Keith circuit. In Chicago, the scene of her earlier triumphs, she broke up the house with *Cold Winter Blues*, *Rampart Street Blues*, *Always Be Careful*, *Mama* and *St Louis Gal*. The beginning of January 1925 saw her featured at the expensive and very exclusive Cotton Club in New York, from where she broadcast three times weekly with Andy Preer and his Cotton Club Syncopators. It was an extremely busy year and work kept rolling in. In November she had formed a band with Fullerton as her musical director. With this group she topped the bill in all the first-run theatres, including the Lincoln, New York. The unit disbanded in February of that year owing to the Keith circuit's failure to obtain consecutive bookings, and once again Miss Hegamin set out as a single, with Fullerton as her pianist. In March she returned to the Lincoln as a featured artist in a revue, Lincoln Frolics. In this production the co-star was Adelaide Hall, another fine singer, who had sung with Duke Ellington's band. In this year her Cameo recording contract came to an end, and she went over to Columbia. For the November session the company gave her, as an accompanying group, a band organised by Clarence Williams who was doing a lot of work for Columbia at the time. Once again her recordings sold well and the outlook was rosy. Thus for a few more years the Hegamin saga ran on, it was blue skies all the way – and then suddenly it was all over, and this great performer disappeared from the scene. Why? Nobody really knows, and I have the impression that Lucille would rather not talk about it. It is quite possible that the death of her husband was the cause, but what is certain is that she no longer had the desire to continue.

Some forty years later she cut some sides for Victoria Spivey's label, and a few titles for Prestige-Bluesville, which showed she was still singing extremely well. The re-make of *He May Be Your Man* is even better than the original version, while *No 12 Train*, composed by Miss Spivey, is quite superb.

Lucille Hegamin reflected the era in which she lived her professional life; she owed far more to vaudeville, from which she emerged, than she did to the formal blues, and her material consisted of a wide variety of songs. It was never her intention to confine herself to one small portion of the musical world. She looked upon herself as a true professional able to cope with anything (within reason) that came her way; as the blues were part of the scene, she sang them, and sang them in her own way. In doing so, her influence on others was considerable. She may have been ignored by present-day critics, but is firmly established in the story of the blues, and with that was content. In her Harlem home she lived happily, working for her local church until the end of 1969. She died in the Harlem Hospital on 1st March, 1970.

Edith Wilson, the third important member of a trio of pioneering women singers, is an artist firmly entrenched in the vaudeville-cabaret tradition, far more so than either Mamie Smith or Lucille

Lucille Hegamin in her Harlem Apartment, 1966.

Hegamin. Her voice is rich and vibrant when heard in person, but to modern ears, the early recordings must sound strange. The clipped phrasing, so typical of the period, is a far cry from the performers we hear in 1970. Yet, amid all the refinement and histrionics, there is hidden deep down in the roots of the blues, another Edith Wilson, a jazz singer, who can shout out a song with feeling and conviction. Unfortunately, she was not served well by the early recording techniques – on many of her best sides she sounds distant, and often overpowered by her accompaniment. As she used Johnny Dunn and his band, every member of which had a great sympathy and understanding for the blues, the fault obviously did not lie with the orchestra. I suspect that her extremely powerful voice was too much for the primitive

27

equipment. Nevertheless, on such items as *Frankie* and *Old Time Blues* and the magnificent *Rules And Regulations, Signed Razor Jim*, she overcomes the difficulties of the studio conditions, and comes roaring through the years. This latter is a most interesting song, and tells the story of a tough, small-time hustler, a promoter of dances, who enforced good conduct by means of his *Rules And Regulations*. This composition by Perry Bradford paints a vivid picture of the gangster in Negro ghettoes during the 'twenties. Miss Wilson sings the lyrics with great relish. On the reverse side she sings a splendid version of Lucille Hegamin's *He May Be Your Man, But He Comes To See Me Sometimes*. Even with the poor quality of the recording, Miss Wilson achieves a minor masterpiece. *I Don't Want Nobody* is another good performance. The Dunn band is in good form and Edith herself proves that she knows just what swing means. The composition is not as good as *Regulations*, but the material is transformed by Miss Wilson; it is very much the case of the singer being much better than the song.

In 1966, when I was in Chicago, Miss Wilson was kind enough to invite me to see her. She lives in a luxurious house in one of the best parts of the city. She proved to be a charming and very attractive hostess, and one who was eager to talk and help in any way she could. She has never looked upon herself as a blues singer, but as an experienced stage artist who, like Lucille Hegamin, is capable of handling a wide variety of roles. In a long and distinguished career she has sung with most of the top-class bands. She appeared with Duke Ellington in one of the big Cotton Club productions, was one of the stars of Blackbirds, has visited Europe six times, and would like to come over once more before she retires.

'I have lived a very full life,' she said, 'and I have been in some wonderful shows. The Plantation Revue was one of the finest and had a number of most talented artists in the huge cast. Another fine one which also came to Europe was Rhapsody In Black, but this was much later, around about 1935. In this show the Sam Wooding Orchestra was featured. This was a very fine group, perhaps the best at the time. It was so versatile and could, literally, play anything. I suppose Hot Chocolates was my happiest experience; just imagine having Louis Armstrong and Fats Waller working with you. Louis and Fats were billed as 1,000 pounds of Harmony. I believe that was supposed to include me!'

Edith Godall (her maiden name) was born in Louisville,

Photograph: Edith Wilson.

May Alix and Edith Wilson Back in U. S.

New York, June 6.—May Alix, Edith Wilson and Henry Sapers arrived here from Paris, France, where they spent most of their time. Miss Alix will most likely return to Chicago, where she will be star of a coming revue in one of the night clubs there.

———————◆———————

Kentucky, and she comes from a very distinguished family. Like so many of the great singers, she began to appreciate music when she was very young, and being an extremely strong-willed young lady, she was determined to make a success of her stage career, for she never had any doubt that when she was old enough she would devote her life to the theatre. Her father was a schoolteacher for over thirty years, and was much respected in the Louisville community. In her spacious living room there hangs a picture of a most distinguished looking black lady who was her great-grandmother; the literary world knows her well without recognising her name, for she was the original model for Liza in Harriet Beecher Stowe's famous novel of slavery, *Uncle Tom's Cabin*. Furthermore, her great-grandfather on her father's side was John C. Breckenridge, a former Vice-President of the United States. 'I am very proud of my family record and I think I have a right to be. I hope that in my own way I have contributed something to American show business', she said. 'It's been a good and happy life, and it's not over yet, I hope. I have played with some of the greatest names in jazz, such as Duke Ellington, and Jimmy Lunceford, and also appeared on Broadway with that wonderful dancer, Bill 'Bojangles' Robinson, surely the greatest hoofer of all time.'

For the past eighteen years Edith Wilson, who married the pianist-composer, Danny Wilson, has been taking the part of Aunt Jemima, the famous character advertising the cookies for the

Quaker Oats programme. For this she has been unfairly criticised by members of her race, who think the role is shameful, but Edith Wilson has no time for this attitude and does not consider Aunt Jemima is in any way 'Uncle Tom'. 'Jemima is a well-loved character – almost a folk figure who gives out love and kindness, so how can that be bad?' she said with some heat.

In 1964 she was made a Kentucky Colonel, the first black artist to receive this honour. Edith Wilson has always been a versatile artist, acting, singing, appearing on television and, of course, on radio. She is perhaps best known for her impersonation of Kingfish's mother-in-law in the Amos and Andy Show, which ran for so many years and was one of the most popular radio features in America. It is hard to imagine this dignified lady in such a role – a very far cry from her blues-based recordings.

In a cabinet in her sitting room she has a pile of songs she has written over the years. I looked through some of these, and found many of them to be most original; they should most certainly be recorded some day. Perhaps it is not too much to hope that with all the recording activities that are going on in the United States, some enterprising company will bring Edith Wilson back to the studio, for assuredly she has not let time catch up with her. Her voice is as good as ever, and she has moved with the changing years. She has been away from all of us far too long.

Illustrations: Edith Wilson in the 'twenties and the 'sixties.

Brief Interlude-
Reflections on Rosa

Rosa Henderson, who died in 1968, was one of the most popular singers of her day. Like her contemporaries, Lucille Hegamin and Edith Wilson, she sang blues, popular songs of the day and the kind of acid blues ballad, well flavoured with humour, which is typical of the period. Her death came as a shock but not as a great surprise. Perhaps it was a merciful release. I met her only once – it was not a very happy occasion. A dull, cheerless day in mid-May, 1966, with a fine drizzle that soaked through the thickest clothes. Not the sort of weather to go visiting a sick friend. The rather seedy Harlem street looked uninviting, and there seemed to be a blight over the whole area. We made our way gingerly up a dark stairway. The door of her apartment was opened by a woman (I never did find out her exact relationship to Rosa, but I believe it was her daughter-in-law). 'She's very sick, but I am sure she would like to see you – it's been so long since anyone remembered her or her records, and when she knows you have come all the way from England, she'll be thrilled; it is sure to cheer her up, and that is what she wants more than anything else. She's very low in spirit,' the woman said.

We were ushered into a large, gloomy, but scrupulously clean bedroom, and there, lying on a bed in a dark corner, was an incredibly frail old lady, obviously very ill indeed. She bore little resemblance to the photographs of the young and pretty girl of the 'twenties – the star of so many records. Alas, time has no respect for beauty. At our entry, her eyes opened, and when she saw Victoria Spivey, who had brought us to Rosa's home, a suggestion of a smile appeared on her lined and careworn face, but it was only a hint, a flash of sunshine, through the gloom.

The next half-hour was one of the most painful experiences of our lives. This once-famous singer was touched by our presence. She just could not get over the fact that we had come all the way from Great Britain and that we should have remembered and loved her records. When we took our leave my wife was close to tears and I was feeling very depressed. We had been talking to a ghost, half in this world and half in some limbo of the lost. She

Rosa Henderson in the mid-'twenties.

had made a supreme effort to entertain us, and I think we had been able for a few brief moments to cheer her up. I had not the heart to ask her all the questions I had in mind. Here was a slice of history, but she was far too ill to think or talk about the past. The real trouble with Rosa was that she lacked the will to live, or fight her illness. She was a heartbroken woman, the death of her husband (some years past, but she had not forgotten) and a personal problem involving a dearly loved relative had taken their toll. She was a shattered old lady when we saw her, yet Leonard Kunstadt, Victoria's manager and friend, assured us that only a few months previously she was still capable of singing extremely well. Now we knew that the end of the road was in sight for poor Rosa Henderson.

The young writer and collector, Bill Daynes-Wood, who has made a study of these early women singers and is particularly fond of Rosa's work, has given us the best critical estimation of Miss Henderson's career. In 'Jazz Journal' he wrote: 'Born in 1896, Rosa Henderson was one of the most outstanding of the early women vaudeville-blues singers to record for the race record companies in the early 'twenties.

'Her recording career covers the span of nine years, from the first for Victor in 1923 to the last for Columbia in 1931. During these years her name appeared on a variety of record labels, including Vocalion, Paramount, Ajax and Edison. Also, nearly a hundred titles appeared under her name and such pseudonyms as Josephine Thomas, Sarah Johnson, and Mamie Harris.

'Her voice was strong, but at the same time possessed a sweet tone. The material she recorded varied from typical vaudeville numbers as *He May Be Your Dog*, *But He's Wearing My Collar Now* and *Hey*, *Hey And He He*, *I'm Charleston Crazy*, to blues like *Penitentiary Bound Blues* and *Back Wood Blues*. Also many of her accompanists were of no mean status, including the complete Fletcher Henderson band, and such names as Coleman Hawkins, Charlie Green, Louis Metcalf, James P. Johnson, and countless others.

'Proof of her popularity with the record buying public was made clear by the number of titles released, and the only reason her recording career was cut short was the death of her husband, Slim. Slim's death left Rosa heartbroken, and she retired from show business altogether.'

If she had lived, she would have made at least one more session, for the suggestion had been put to her, and she seemed anxious to do it. However, it was not to be. Further news of the relative who was giving her so much worry brought on a rapid deterioration in her health. I'm glad we saw her before she died.

14652 —If You Don't Give Me What I Want
Rosa Henderson
—So Long To You and the Blues ..Rosa Henderson

10 in.   **$.75**

The Classic Blues-
Southern Style

In 1923, two women, Ma Rainey and Bessie Smith, were responsible for a change of taste among that section of the black population who were buying blues based records. This change was not produced in an instant, but took place over a number of years. As we have seen, until the advent of Rainey and Smith, the accent had been on the smooth, refined sophistication of Lucille Hegamin and Edith Wilson, plus the imitators who cashed in on their popularity, even to the extent of making 'covers' of their songs for rival companies.

With Ma Rainey came the sounds of the South, the blues of the field workers (or their later derivatives), the songs of the wandering musicians and the ballads of the tent and minstrel shows. This is what Ma Rainey offered on her records; she and Bessie were responsible for the great change that was to take place. It came slowly at first, but with increasing speed in later years.

Although Bessie Smith preceded her in the studio by a few months, it was the older woman who was the most important at the outset. In this chapter we must attempt to penetrate the world in which these women lived, and endeavour to trace their musical lives.

The history of the blues is surrounded by myth and legend, for collectors, in the main, are incurable romantics, although few will admit this fact. This romanticism encourages the birth of fables and fairy stories. Undoubtedly, this makes for colourful writing, but it does not help the earnest researcher to reach the truth. Even now, after many years of painstaking detective work by dedicated men, the complete and accurate story of Ma Rainey has yet to be told. There are many gaps to be filled and we can but hope that it is not too late. With the available data, writers and critics can only speculate and resort to inspired guesses. Investigation into the background of these artists, the tent shows, the black variety circuits, such as T.O.B.A, is long overdue, but it is unlikely that we shall ever know the full story of this most fascinating side of the musical scene. The writer and critic, Charles Edward Smith, has done invaluable work. In fact, the

35

greater part of the Rainey story that has been printed in magazine articles and on the back of LP sleeves has come from Mr Smith's continual probing into the past. Seldom has he received acknowledgement from those who have used his material.

Unlike pop music, jazz and blues (the two cannot be separated) is a very personal art, therefore it follows that the more we know about its practitioners, the better we will understand their music. The pop star, on the other hand, is more often than not merely a robot, turning off and on, rushing to embrace each new gimmick as it appears, and, as what he sings is ephemeral and trivial, he reflects nothing but a useless void. The blues singer is entirely different, for he is very much involved with what he (or she) is doing, and the music he makes and sings is unconsciously moulded to his own way of living and feeling. This involvement is a genuine and basic part of the music, so to learn something about the background of these artists is important.

Although Ma Rainey's history is somewhat short in detail, we can obtain some idea as to her personality and her influence on those who followed her. The facts are these: Gertrude Pridgett Rainey was a Georgia woman, and she was born on April 26th, 1886, in Columbus. Her early years were uneventful, very much like any other little black girl of her class. Her father, Thomas Pridgett, and her mother, Ella Allen, came originally from Alabama, and moved to Columbus before she was born. One of her grandmothers was on the stage in the years after Emancipation, and it is probably from her that the young girl inherited her love and talent for show business. There was another daughter, Melissa, and a brother, Tom Pridgett Jr; rumour also has it that Tom and Ella had two other children of whom no details are forthcoming, but as they do not seem to have been connected in any way with the stage, they do not enter into this story.

Gertrude's interest and passion for the theatre developed early in her life, and by 1900 she had made her debut at the local Opera House in a talent show called The Bunch of Blackberries. No newspaper reviews of this production have been traced, so we have no idea of what she did or how she fared. Presumably she did well enough and was encouraged to proceed with her chosen career.

The next date of note is February 2nd, 1904, when she married another performer, William 'Pa' Rainey, and for many years they had their own song and dance routine in various minstrel shows. All over the south she travelled, and her fame among her race

"MA" RAINEY

"Mother of the Blues"

Recognized as the greatest Blues Singer ever known. Her records are breaking all records for popularity. "Ma" is the Mother of the Blues, because she really taught many of the younger stars how to sing Blues. They call "Ma" Rainey the gold-neck woman of the Blues because of her necklace of twenty-dollar gold pieces. But it's her golden voice, also, that has earned her the title. She's the only Blues singer of the Race elevated to the title of "Madame".

12200—THE FAMOUS MYSTERY RECORD Acc. Lovie Austin's Blues Serenaders   **Madam "Ma" Rainey**
HONEY WHERE YOU BEEN SO LONG Acc. Lovie Austin's Ser-
enaders   **Madam "Ma" Rainey**

12098—DREAM BLUES Acc. Two Guitars, Pruett Twins **Madam "Ma" Rainey**

LOST WANDERING BLUES Acc. Two Guitars, Pruett Twins
                                                       Madam "Ma" Rainey

More "Ma" Rainey Records on Next Page

Above: Gertrude 'Ma' Rainey was already considered the greatest of the women singers when she commenced to record.

was almost legendary. For many months she was with the celebrated Rabbit Foot Minstrels. She must have looked an impressive sight, this squat, rather heavy-featured woman, dressed in an imposing gown covered with sequins which sparkled and shone in the kerosene footlights, her necklace and ear medallions fashioned from gold coins. She was usually accompanied by a jug band (they were very popular at the time), or a more orthodox jazz band consisting of five or six musicians. From all accounts hers was not a big voice, it was at times, harsh, but it was ideally suited to her simple songs of everyday life, and her driving 'down home' blues. It was when she and Will Rainey were with Tolliver's Circus and Musical Extravaganza that the pair were billed as 'Rainey and Rainey, Assassinators Of The Blues', a title indicative of the style of the act, which contained comedy, dancing and songs. She remained with the Tolliver Circus for two years (1914–1916). It may seem strange to find a blues singer working in a circus, and it would appear that many besides Ma Rainey did join the Big Top in those early years. How and when were they used? This has always been a question that has puzzled researchers. Perhaps the following information supplied by circus authority, Ken Lane, may supply the answer. In an effort to squeeze the last dollar from the public, the management would put on what they called 'The After Show' (for which extra was charged). The band would come out front and give a 'musical entertainment', and it is more than possible that it was here that our singers were featured. Mr Lane hastens to add that he can find no trace of any such artists mentioned on his numerous play-bills, nor do his records tell us much, but if singers were part of the company (as we know they were) this is obviously the ideal place for them.

The Freak Shows, which were part of the unit, were very different from the British ones. Apart from the Fat Lady, the Giants, Midgets, the Limbless Woman or the Alligator Skin Boy, the show had a number of 'acts' which could not be considered freaks at all, consisting of conjurors, Punch and Judy, and Sword Swallowers. It is possible, though unlikely, that singers were also included.

It is interesting to note that Gertrude Rainey was one of the last of the great Negro minstrel artists, and definitely one of the first to feature blues as such (around 1902) on the stage. With these songs she reached her highest peak, which lasted through-

Opposite: Madame 'Ma' Rainey, the 'Gold Necklace Woman of the Blues,' as she was billed on tour. Overleaf: 'Ma' Rainey on stage with her Georgia Jazz Band, including Ed Pollack (trumpet), Al Wynn (trombone) and Georgia Tom (piano). The Paramount Eagle was painted on the stage backdrop.

out the 'twenties. The managers for whom she worked and the productions in which she featured during her career were many and varied. Silas Green, Al Gaines and C. W. Parks are perhaps the best known. She also had her own shows, touring always in the Southern States, although when she made her records – mostly in Chicago – she would sing her blues to Northern audiences. Nevertheless, her heart was in the South, where her people knew and loved her.

Champion Jack Dupree, who saw her frequently, remembers her well and he gave me this brief word-picture of what it was like to experience her performance: 'She was really an ugly woman', Jack related, 'but when she opened her mouth – that was it! You forgot everything. She knew how to sing those blues, and she got right into your heart. What a personality she had. One of the greatest of all singers.'

The Negro poet, Sterling Brown, who was lecturing at Fiske University also recalled seeing the great singer. In a taped interview with Paul Oliver he gave his impressions: 'Ma Rainey was a tremendous figure. She wouldn't have to sing any words; she would moan, and the audience would moan with her. She had them in the palm of her hand. I heard Bessie Smith also, but Ma Rainey was the greatest mistress of an audience. Bessie was the greater blues singer, but Ma really *knew* these people; she was a person of the folk; she was very simple and direct. That night when we saw her, she was having boy trouble. You see, she liked these young musicians, and in comes John Work and I – we were young to her. We were something sent down, and she didn't know which one to choose. Each of us knew we were not choosing her! We just wanted to talk, but she was interested in other things. She was that direct. She was the tops for my money. She was all right.'

She knew she was a blues queen, and like so many others who followed here, she acted the part. Ma was volcanic and spoke her mind, though underneath her apparent sternness, she was soft-hearted and generous; but she was a tigress when roused. A picture is now beginning to emerge; a picture of a woman fond of flashy jewellery and striking clothes. A warm-hearted, generous human being, wrapped up in the world of the theatre; the vaudeville stage with its songs, and the blues of her race were very much part of her. All the toughness of her life and character is there in her singing.

Paramount, for whom she recorded, was primarily a blues

label and the blues were becoming popular and selling well to the southern folk. Therefore, all they wanted from her was blues or blues based songs. Thus we obtain a false impression of the range of her talent. According to reports of those who saw her and knew her well, she had many accomplishments.

One of the great drawbacks when playing early records is the quality of the recording and the scratchy surfaces which greatly hinder appreciation of the music. Luckily many re-issues of these ancient discs have been cleaned up, and with the aid of modern techniques we are able to get a good idea of how she sounded in person. Of the ninety-odd titles she made there are many gems, and few could be considered poor. Those made with Louis Armstrong are particularly fine. Tommy Ladnier also cut some fine sides with Ma, and these two musicians are among the greatest of all blues accompanists.

The three blues with Louis – *Counting The Blues*, *Jelly Bean Blues* and *See See Rider* – are all splendid examples of Rainey's style, and the youthful Armstrong, only twenty-three at that time, plays some very sensitive cornet. *See See Rider* is perhaps the outstanding performance. The debt she owes to vaudeville can be heard in her duets with the medicine show singer, Papa Charlie Jackson, *Ma And Pa's Poorhouse Blues* and *Big Feeling Blues*. The former is full of backchat and music hall hokum. It is a most satisfying package of blues and humour.

All the titles with Tommy Ladnier can be recommended. Particularly worthy of note are *Cell Bound Blues*, a very grim blues in which Ladnier's horn combines with Jimmy O'Bryant's clarinet to provide a wonderfully sympathetic backing to the

Paramount
ELECTRICALLY   RECORDED
12718-A   Vocal
                         Banjo Acc.

Ma and Pa Poorhouse Blues
Ma Rainey and
Papa Charlie Jackson
20921

THE NEW YORK RECORDING LABORATORIES · PORT WASHINGTON, WIS.

voice. Ladnier is most impressive on *Bo-Weavil Blues*; his growling comments and final lead in the last chorus are most striking, and Ma is obviously inspired to give of her best.

Ma's last numbers were recorded for Paramount on December 28th, 1928. An official of the company told Charles Edward Smith that 'Ma's down-home material had gone out of fashion'. Be that as it may, Gertrude Rainey did not enter a recording studio after the two duets with Papa Charlie Jackson already mentioned. She continued to work for some time after this, but on the death of her sister, Malissa, in 1935 and the death of her mother a few months later, she returned to the home she had built for her family from her earnings. Her later years were spent running two theatres she had acquired in Columbus and Rome, Georgia, the Lyric and Airdrome. She also joined the Congregation of Friendship Baptist Church, of which her brother, Thomas Pridgett Jr, was a deacon. She died in 1939, and is buried in the family plot in Porterdale Cemetery, Columbus.

Her death came just when collectors and critics were beginning to appreciate her. Unlike Bessie Smith, she never became popular in the North, where her work was almost unknown (until her records began to filter into the big cities such as Chicago), but in the South she was loved and respected by her own folk, and her influence on other singers was considerable. Until Bessie Smith became the universal symbol of the Classic Blues, Ma Rainey reigned supreme.

There is little need to recount the life story of Bessie Smith. It has been told numberless times and must be familiar to most blues lovers. Paul Oliver's book on her gave all the authenticated details. Therefore, it is only necessary to concentrate on a few important incidents in her career.

Bessie was born on April 15th, 1898, at Chattanooga, Tennessee, of poor parents, and when she was very young she showed a great talent for the stage, appearing frequently in school plays. Even in those early schooldays she had a fine voice, and when she was only nine she made her professional debut at the Ivory Theatre in her home town.

Opinions differ as to just when (and precisely where) her meeting with Gertrude 'Ma' Rainey took place. Charles Edward Smith tells us it was when Rainey was working with the Tolliver Circus and Tent Show. Paul Oliver states it was when Ma was with the

Bessie Smith at the commencement of her career.
44

BESSIE SMITH
"The Empress of Blues"

WHEREVER blues are sung, there will you hear the name of Bessie Smith, best loved of all the Race's great blues singers. Bessie has the knack of picking the songs you like and the gift of singing them the way you want them sung. Every year this famous "Empress of Blues" tours the country, appearing before packed houses.

Miss Smith is an exclusive Columbia Artist

BESSIE SMITH
"The Empress of Blues"

SEND ME TO THE 'LECTRIC CHAIR— *Accompanied by Her Blue Boys* . . . THEM'S GRAVEYARD WORDS—*Accompanied by Her Blue Boys*	14209-D	75c
MUDDY WATER (A Mississippi Moan)— *Accompanied by Her Band* . . . . AFTER YOU'VE GONE—*Accompanied by Her Band*	14197-D	75c
BACK-WATER BLUES . . . . . PREACHIN' THE BLUES—*Piano Accompaniments by Jimmy Johnson*	14195-D	75c
YOUNG WOMAN'S BLUES—*Accompanied by Her Blue Boys* . . . . . . HARD TIME BLUES—*Piano Accompaniment by Fletcher Henderson*	14179-D	75c
ONE AND TWO BLUES—*Accompanied by Her Blue Boys* . . . . HONEY MAN BLUES—*Piano Accompaniment by Fletcher Henderson*	14172-D	75c

Columbia Records announce 'The Empress of the Blues.'

Rabbit Foot Minstrels. To the historian, this must be frustrating, but for our purpose it is sufficient that they *did* meet. We can only guess at the date, but it must have been between 1913 and 1916. Her status with the company was small. Madame Rainey was the star of the show. Paul Oliver has given a brief description of her act: 'During the course of the next few years Bessie Smith was well featured in the "Rabbit Foot" show as a child singer in short skirts, and she improved all the while.'

It has often been said that Ma was Bessie's teacher, but this statement should be regarded with caution: blues singers are born, not taught. They learn the art of presentation and showmanship by hard work and gradual experience. Moreover, Ma Rainey was a proud woman, proud of being a blues queen. It is inconceivable that she would train a girl so talented, and far more likely that she would look upon her as a potential rival. That being said, we can look at Bessie in a less romantic light. It is quite obvious that Bessie was very much influenced by what she heard. It is apparent in all her early recordings, and this great influence never left her. The debt she owed is plain. After all, a sensitive young girl learning her job is bound to be impressed with such an artist, and the admiration she held for her was to remain for the rest of her too-short life. Perhaps the true importance of Gertrude Rainey was not the impact of her records on a section of the public, but the fact that Bessie Smith met and worked with her.

As the years went by Bessie began to blossom, and from her first record, made on February 16th, 1923, *Downhearted Blues* and *Gulf Coast Blues*, it was apparent that here was a new star. Rough and down to earth, this woman seemed as if she was out to prove to herself and everyone that she was going to be the greatest of all singers. From all accounts her personality was aggressive (and this quality can be heard in her singing). She was a complex person, on the one hand generous to a fault when she had the money, on the other, mean and unkind to other artists. She was childlike on occasion, but she could be extremely sharp and alert if she thought she had been wronged.

At the peak of her career she was a breathtaking performer, and she transformed what we now call the Classic Blues into a fresh and intriguing vocal expression. Her achievement was, I believe, unconscious; with her natural genius she took the vaudeville style of singing, the country blues form, and certain jazz elements, and these she moulded into a perfect whole. The result was a completely original art form. Quite apart from this amazing feat, her singing was very subtle: underneath the superficial excitement of that magnificent, rich contralto, there was subtlety of timing and phrasing that the casual listener could easily miss. She used her vocal resources to the full. Her voice was an instrument and she gave fresh value to almost every note she sang, bending it to her will; at times she would glide down on her top notes, dropping them down an octave. Her suspension and timing was amazing, and her habit of dragging over a word or a syllable into the next bar was copied by many others. The late Billie Holiday has admitted that Bessie Smith was one of her greatest influences; it was her phrasing that inspired Billie, and which she used (and altered) as a basis for her style.

Bessie's repertoire was extensive, but in her early and middle years she concentrated on blues. She sang of privation, of bad luck and bad women, of good men. Her song *Back Water Blues* was a classic and has been recorded countless times by singers both male and female. The glorious *Hot Spring Blues*, with Joe Smith's beautiful cornet, is one of the many gems of her recorded career. Like Ma Rainey, she used some of the best jazz musicians of the era. It would be true to say that nearly every musician of quality was on her sessions from 1923 to her final date in 1933.

On the Columbia four volume set much of her great work is included. Volume 1 is devoted to titles she made with Louis Armstrong. The January 24th, 1925, session was a superb example of Classic Blues. Louis and Fred Longshaw, on piano and organ, play with great understanding. *St Louis Blues*, *You've Been A Good Ole Wagon* and *Cold In Hand* are perhaps the best of a wonderful batch. On May 26th and 27th in the same year, with Charlie Green's trombone added, four more blues of outstanding quality were recorded: *Careless Love*, *Nashville Woman Blues*, *I Ain't Gonna Play No Second Fiddle* and *J. C. Holmes Blues*. It would be quite impossible to choose a single number from this group of songs. All are beautifully integrated performances, and Armstrong and Green give ideal support. The same high praise can be given to almost every title on the four LPs, but I have only room to mention a few of these musical gems. Volume 2 contains the famous *Nobody Knows You When You're Down And Out*. This is surely too well known to warrant more than a mention. It is sufficient to say that this is the best performance of this very good song of poverty. With popular songs from the vaudeville stage or minstrel shows she was superb, transforming them into blues. Examples can be heard on Volume 3. *Cake Walking*

Above: Bessie Smith in performance in the late 'twenties.

Babies, a ragtime song, and *Baby Doll*, direct from the music hall, are beautiful performances. They become fresh compositions when Bessie interprets them. Here can be detected the merging of all the influences of which I have written.

Two numbers on Volume 2 have tragic implications, for they tell a real-life story: *Me And My Gin* and *Gin House Blues*.

These are both grim blues on the subject of alcohol, and by this time Bessie was drinking heavily; the pace at which she was living, and the tensions of trying to keep on the top of the pile, were in part the cause. Nevertheless, she was still singing superbly; but the constant fear of slipping and the frantic life she was leading were taking their toll. The voice, still marvellous, was taking on a coarser quality, and she was trying desperately to widen her appeal. With this in mind, she broadened her material, and such risqué, double-entendre songs as *Kitchen Man, You've Got To Give Me Some* and *I'm Wild About That Thing* were recorded. In all fairness, this sort of song has always been part of the blues, and these are good examples of their type which Miss Smith sings extremely well. Furthermore, side by side with these items there was still some very fine material; *Black Mountain Blues* on Volume 4 and *In The House Blues* show that she could still sing with telling conviction.

Time was running out for Bessie Smith, and, like other artists, she faded into obscurity with the Depression of 1930. In 1933, John Hammond brought her back into the studio with a hand-picked band of star musicians including Benny Goodman, Jack Teagarden, Frankie Newton, Chu Berry and Buck Washington. A mixture of styles, but it worked. Newton on trumpet and Teagarden on trombone are the men most in sympathy with Bessie, and they carry her along with ease. These four titles (on Volume 1 of the Columbia set) were as good as anything she had ever recorded; *Take Me For A Buggy Ride, Gimme A Pigfoot, Do Your Duty* and *I'm Down In The Dumps* proved that she was still a vital force. The future looked bright and she had another session lined up. Alas, it was not to be. On Sunday morning September 26th, 1937, while speeding down the highway near Coahoma, Mississippi, in her car, she crashed into the back of a lorry. Bessie was terribly mutilated, one arm almost torn from her body. There has been a great deal written about what happened after the crash, and many conflicting stories told. Some say she bled to death on the sidewalk as no hospital would take her in because of her colour. Another version is that she died from exposure in a hospital waiting room while awaiting attention. Yet another says that while a passing doctor was trying to lift this heavy woman into his car, his vehicle was struck by on-coming traffic and completely wrecked. An ambulance arrived and took her to the

Left: Bessie Smith at Carl van Vetchten's studio, about 1932.

Negro Ward of the nearest hospital, the G. T. Thomas Hospital at Clarksdale. There she died of her injuries around mid-day. This is probably the true version.

In the 'Esquire' magazine for June 1969, there appeared an article on Bessie Smith, which contained an interview with the doctor who attended her at the scene of the accident. Dr Hugh Smith confirmed most of the details, he also stated that in his opinion nothing more could have been done to save her life. Besides her dreadful arm injury, grave enough in itself, she was bleeding internally. Everything possible was done to save her life. The only obscure question now remains is, exactly where did she die? Was it in the ambulance? Was it by the roadside (the doctor is rather vague on this point), or was it at the hospital? The G.T. Thomas hospital is no longer in existence, so it is useless to expect any information from that source. However, whichever version one accepts, it makes little difference to the tragic fact that one of the greatest Negro performers died many years before her time, and the jazz and blues world lost one of its finest singers. She was called 'The Empress of the Blues'; never was a title so richly deserved.

A still from the short, St. Louis Blues, *the only film in which Bessie Smith appeared.*

Wild Women Get the Blues...

Only show business, and vaudeville in particular, could have created such an unbelievable character as Ida Cox. Certainly no author would have dared to invent her, and if he had done so, he would never have put such a wildly improbable person into a book.

All the blues queens were larger than life, most of them carried the regal myth into their everyday lives. Their fans were their subjects, the musicians and their managers were their cabinet ministers, there to pander to their will, and surprisingly enough, they did just that! Thus, for part of the time they lived in a world of their own, a world of fantasy and daydream.

To this extravagant world Ida Cox belonged, and throughout her highly successful career she insisted on being treated with the respect due to a queen. Although the critics have done her less than justice, for she worked in the shadow of Ma Rainey and Bessie Smith, her many records for the Paramount company were best-sellers, and, together with Ma Rainey, she was the main attraction this company had to offer in the race market; the more down-to-earth male singers were to become popular at a later date.

Ida was much more sophisticated and more firmly rooted in vaudeville than either Rainey or Smith. Perhaps this is the reason she never really attracted the jazz and blues writers. Yet there is no mistaking her country origin, it is there in her singing for all to hear. Her voice was lighter and not so rich as Ma's, but much of her artistry is lost by the early recording.

Information is scanty concerning her early life. She was born in Knoxville, Tennessee, around 1900 or maybe a little earlier, and was the first of the Paramount blues artists, her first session being in June 1923, six months before Gertrude Rainey. From this first date until her last Paramount session in October 1929, she produced a series of consistently good records. Their subject matter varied from the grim *Coffin Blues*, with King Oliver on cornet and Jessee Crump on piano, to her own composition, the more light-hearted *Mean Papa Turn Your Key*. Most of her songs

53

were interesting, both melodically and lyrically. *Bone Orchard Blues*, for example, with its gloomy overtones of death ('Bone Orchard' being the cemetery), or one of her most attractive and famous songs, *Wild Women Don't Have The Blues*; but there were many more, some of the best of which were composed by Jessee Crump, her accompanist for many years. She was a prolific composer herself, and besides those already mentioned, she also wrote *Fogyism*, a most interesting blues dealing with superstition, common among the Southern country workers; *Western Union Blues*, on the theme of the rejected woman, and *Tree Top Tall Papa*, the saga of an unfaithful lover.

Like all Classic Blues singers, both vaudeville and country style, Ida Cox preferred to have top-class jazz musicians working with her, and a glance at her discography will show that she used some of the best jazzmen on her dates; men such as King Oliver, Tommy Ladnier, Dave Nelson, Jessee Crump and Jimmy O'Bryant were regular participants.

It cannot be said that she influenced anyone. She was herself and sang about what interested her, and it would appear that other artists kept their distance, for Ida could cut her rivals down to size. Tough she might have been, but she was greatly admired, for all her tantrums. As one singer said: 'She was herself – and there was nobody else quite like her. She had her own thing going, and you just couldn't imitate that!'

Being a blues queen she lived, for much of the time, in an imaginary world of her own making. She thought herself above the rules of society. Like a child, that which she fancied she had to have. There was no thought in her mind that what she did might be dishonest. There is an amusing true story that illustrates the point. Ida was renowned as a collector of 'unconsidered trifles', and on one occasion she was playing a theatre somewhere in the Southern States. Her presence in the theatre was regarded with some awe. Having set her sights on a rather magnificent drape which was part of the set furnishings, she sent a boy to take it down so that she could take it home to add another trophy to her Aladdin's cave. The boy was so petrified of her imposing presence that he promptly dealt with her command. That night there was some confusion in the wings when the stage manager was heard to call repeatedly for 'Curtain No. 3', but despite the all-out efforts of the stage staff, nothing was produced but a blank backstage wall!

Victoria Spivey remembers her with affection and no little

IDA COX

"The Uncrowned Queen of the Blues"

You all know Ida. Some call her "The Blues Singer with a Feeling." Others say she is the greatest Blues singer there ever was. We say she is the "Uncrowned Queen of the Blues." There never was a Blues singer who had such a sudden rise to fame as Ida. She seems to get such a world of feeling in her Blues. As one of her admirers said—"Take my house, take my clothes, but don't take away those Blues Ida Cox sang!" You will feel the same way.

12202—**CHICAGO MONKEY MAN**   **Ida Cox and Her Blues Serenaders**
      WORRIED ANY HOW BLUES   **Ida Cox and Her Blues Serenaders**

12094—**MEAN LOVIN' MAN** Acc. Banjo and Guitar
                              Ida Cox and the Pruett Twins
      DOWN THE ROAD BOUND BLUES Acc. Banjo and Guitar
                              Ida Cox and the Pruett Twins

12097—**MEAN PAPA TURN IN YOUR KEY** Acc. Lovie Austin and Her Blues
      Serenaders   **Ida Cox**
      IF YOU SHEIK ON YOUR MAMA Acc. Lovie Austin and Her Blues
      Serenaders   **Edmonia Henderson**

Ida Cox, 'Blues singer with a feeling', publicised in 1924.

amusement. In her Brooklyn apartment, she often talked about those bygone days. 'I first met Ida Cox,' she said, 'in Houston, Texas in 1925. Ida wanted to bring me out of Houston, but something happened that night, and they left without me. I cried all that night because she didn't take me.

'I didn't get to meet her again until 1928 in Chicago. By then I had made it. I was playing at the Metropolitan Theatre. She walked into a big agent's when I happened to be there. She wanted me to go into her company. She offered me good money, and she had a pocket book as big as I was. She had this wide, beautiful hat on, and I wanted to wear clothes like she had. What a dresser she was. If these modern girls would put on a dress like they wore in those days, I think they would have to nail them to the floor. Seven to fifteen hundred dollars was nothing for a petticoat, and I'm not lying. For a head-piece she wore crowns, jewels, and feathers. Those jewels were no fakes, they were *real*!

'Her show was *big* – there was nothing she missed. She had everything. She had sixteen chorus girls kickin' them up. I tell you, she was one of the greatest singers; I can imitate, but I dare not even touch her. As I said, she was sweet all right, but she did not want anyone else to sing blues on her shows. She said to me: "You just sing *Lady Be Good*, *I'm* the blues singer in this show".'

'Ida always had plenty of everything. Anyone would have money if she took everything she found like she always did! She lived in a mansion way out in Tennessee. She put her daughter through college and everything. Her daughter is a big lady today. I never saw Ida hungry in my life. She had so many Traveller Cheques

Below: Ida Cox's road shows, including her celebrated 'Raisin' Cain' Company, followed a tempestuous course across the South. Local reports and letters from the chorus girls marked the trail in 1929. Right: Ida Cox at her last recording session in 1961.

Ida Cox Complains of Untrue Rumors

Dallas, Tex., Jan. 3.—Ida Cox and her "Raisin' Cain" company are in their second week at the Central theater with Miss Cox slightly peeved because she says the show which preceded her gave out the rumor that she would not be with the show when it played here. Miss Cox states she hasn't missed a show this season.

With the production are Jesse Crump and his Six Whoopee Makers, Charles Anderson, David Wiles, Billiken Grimes, Ella Mae Waters Frances Hereford, Billy and Willie Mae, Esther Jackson, Leon Claxton and nine brownskins in the fast chorus.

Little Ethel Jackson writes from the Ida Cox company and says th the show is still "Raisin' Cain." This is their third week at the Central of Dallas, Tex. Well, one is certain they used their summer frocks Xmas while we played in four feet of snow.

Daisy ("Little Bits") Randolph says that she is still raising cain with Ida Cox and her "Raisin' Cain" company. Week of the 18th finds "Bits" at the Frolic theater, Birmingham. "Bits" says that she loves to write and really wants to hear from Ada Chatman. Ella Mae Waters and Mildred Williams. All right, girls, write here quickly now.

An open confession is good for the soul, and it always should do us good when we openly express our thanks

in her bosom, I thought she had a suitcase up there! She carried four or five thousand dollars up there. I know 'cause I used to look at her.

'It's funny how collectors want to know about records. In those days Ida, like me, just made them and forgot all about it. If we had known the interest that those things would arouse today, we would have paid more attention. We just wanted to sing that stuff. We didn't care about anything else, but I do remember I used to practise two of Ida's songs, *Cherry Pickin' Blues* and *Moanin' the Blues.*'

It is interesting to note that they placed so little importance on their records. This seems to suggest that they earned their big money with their stage shows. Discs were probably the jam on the bread. Furthermore, they rarely saw the royalties that were due to them.

Ida's recording career for Paramount ended in 1929, although she continued working for some time after this. In fact she was one of the few Classic Blues singers to work right through until the late 'thirties. In 1939 she came out of semi-retirement to make some sides with an all-star band that included 'Hot Lips' Page on trumpet, J. C. Higginbotham, trombone, and James P. Johnson at the piano. These contain some splendid material and for the first time the recording did justice to her voice. *Death Letter Blues* and *Hard Time Blues* were truly great performances, with Page playing extremely fine horn, reminding one of the halcyon days of the Classic Blues.

In 1940, she returned again, supported by a similar accompanying band with the late Henry Allen on trumpet and Cliff Jackson on piano. This session, too, was artistically successful and at least two of the titles are the equal of anything Miss Cox ever recorded: *Last Mile Blues*, a sombre blues dealing with that last walk to the electric chair, and in a happier vein, *I Can't Quit That Man*, a blues ballad which recalled the old vaudeville songs which Ida loved so well.

In 1961, a very old woman, she was persuaded to make one more date in the studio. Once again the band was star-studded: Coleman Hawkins, Roy Eldridge and Sammy Price were among those who attended. Hawkins and Eldridge play extremely well, but the album, *Blues For Rampart Street*, should never have been made. Age had at last damped the fire, and Ida's voice had lost its edge and sparkle. Her sense of timing had deserted her, and she seemed unsure of some of the lyrics. This was her sad swan song. Her death in 1967 passed almost unnoticed by the musical press.

Victoria Spivey is a remarkable woman. At an age when most people are thinking about a quiet retirement, this human volcano is bounding with energy. Still actively involved in music, she has her own record company (Spivey), and is busy composing songs, searching for new talent, and engaged in recording the surviving Classic Blues ladies. In the last few years she has brought back to the microphone such artists as Lucille Hegamin, Alberta Hunter and Hannah Sylvester, while her catalogue includes such names as Little Brother Montgomery, Memphis Slim, Roosevelt Sykes, Homewick James, Big Joe Williams, Otis Spann and the Muddy Waters Blues Band. In addition to all this, she still appears at concerts throughout the country. It is no mean feat for a woman in her mid-sixties.

To meet Victoria is to encounter a woman of incredible drive and enthusiasm. It can also be an exhausting experience, for she can, and does, reduce one to a helpless wreck in a few days. While her victim is trying vainly to recover, she is still firing on all cylinders. How she is able to carry on, without either rest or sleep, is one of life's unsolved mysteries. When her time comes, Miss Spivey will not die, she will explode.

For as long as she can remember, she has been in show business, and there is not a single angle of the entertainment industry that she does not know. She is, in every sense of the word, a professional. This fascinating woman with her ever-changing moods from grave to gay, is a constant surprise to the onlooker. There is never a dull moment when one is in her company. All these seemingly trivial details may seem irrelevant, but it is this constant and ceaseless energy, together with a great zest for life, that contribute so largely to the quality and style of her compositions. Victoria Spivey is a typical example of a Blues Queen; to study her is to learn about the other performers, from her we can obtain an insight into the neglected past.

As a composer of blues she is, with her fellow Texan, Lightnin' Hopkins, the finest living exponent. Her songs lack the poetic beauty of Hopkins. Whereas Lightnin' will make up a blues on the spot on any subject that takes his fancy and is topical, Miss Spivey likes to take her time, carefully planning her songs before actually writing them. Moreover, poetic beauty is not her aim: much of her work is stark, grim reality, dealing with life at its roughest. A large proportion of her blues is deeply felt and far

from happy. *T.B.Blues*, for example, a song that has been a standard blues for many years, was written when Victoria was at her lowest and its theme of illness haunts one long after the record has finished playing. Her more recent compositions show the same sombre gloom – *Brooklyn Bridge*, a blues tone poem and a masterly musical picture of this famous landmark, has suicide as its main theme. *From Broadway to 7th Avenue* on the same LP is almost frightening in its intensity; here are all the horrors of the alcoholic and drug world, painted with a master brush. Miss Spivey's Texas-style piano and Eddie Barefield's alto underline

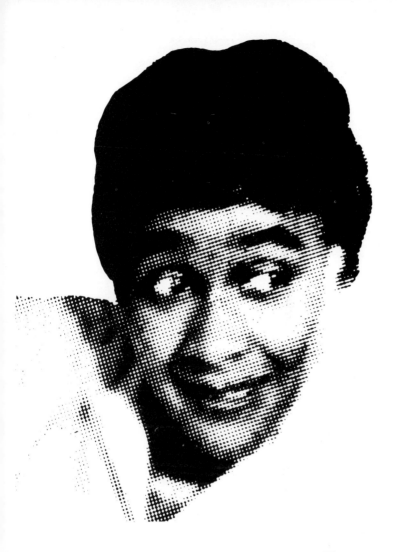

Above: Victoria Spivey when she made her famous T.B. Blues.

the tragedy of the situation.

Victoria can be sadistic too: *Black Belt* is a song which has flogging as its subject and must be one of the most cruel blues ever written. Her world-famous *Black Snake Blues* is, by no stretch of the imagination, a cosy love song. It has richly sexual overtones, and is a classic of its kind. With all her gay chatter, Victoria Spivey is essentially a serious woman and her music reflects this quality. She can, of course, be light-hearted, as in the song she composed for Hannah Sylvester, *Mr Cab*, but it will be noticed that underneath the humorous lyric is a hint of savagery:

> Hurry Mr Cab, I don't want that door shut in my face *(twice)*
> I love New York, can't live no other place.
>
> He said he would be in by twelve, not twelve-o-five   *(twice)*
> Now if I'm late he sure gonna tan my hide.
>
> Mr Cab, slow your motor down, *(twice)*
> I'm gonna throw him out of the window, catch him before he hits the ground!

The apparently light-hearted *Big Black Limousine* from the same LP has an underlying menace, for the Black Limousine turns out to be a hearse!

> You think you're smart for the things you do to me,
> But this big fat insurance you never did see.
> When you shut your eyes and go to sleep
> I'm gonna fix you and ain't gonna weep.
> There's a big black limousine waiting to carry you away!

Most of her songs are little cameos of life, but seldom cosy or comforting. Victoria knows only too well that the world is not made up of sugar and spice. She has been through the mill, and it is of this she sings more often than not. She is cynical at times, sordid too, but these are genuine songs, not synthetic trivia for a plastic age.

It is most fortunate that examples of her early work at a time when she was reaching her peak – a peak she has never left – have been re-issued on her own label. Besides a fine version of *Black Snake*, there is a classic interpretation of *Organ Grinder Blues*. We are indeed lucky to be able to enjoy Miss Spivey's art to the full; from ancient to modern, it is all available.

Her voice lacks the richness and depth of Bessie Smith's, but it has an acid, biting quality admirably suited to her down-to-earth blues. As with all the classic singers, her vaudeville connections are plainly heard. She stayed in St Louis for several years, and the peculiar vocal tones of the female St Louis singers can be traced; in fact Miss Spivey strides over into St Louis territory at times. In her can be heard echoes of Louise and Mary

Above: Victoria Spivey today.

Johnson, Alice Moore and the small group of lady singers from that city who had so much in common when it came to singing the blues. Her career spans the years, but she is ageless and timeless. Her fight to preserve the Classic Blues has met with success. She is rightly called 'Queen Victoria'.

Queens of the Moaners

Clara Smith's whole life is shrouded in mystery, and that is possibly the reason for the neglect that has been shown by both collectors and critics of whom few are familiar with her work. The lack of detail on Miss Smith is unfortunate, as she is a most intriguing and fascinating artist who left behind her on record almost the complete story of her artistic progress; from the inexperienced beginner to the self-assured and very good singer of her later discs. A study of these records will show how quickly she matured. Her first recordings were made in 1923, and her last in 1932, but by early 1925, or even late 1924, she was a vastly different singer, much more of a blues artist, and closer to her more distinguished namesake.

So obscure is her history that even her birth-place is uncertain. Clyde Bernhardt, in a letter to Bill Daynes-Wood, is probably correct when he writes: 'Clara was born in Spartanberg, South Carolina, in 1895; that is what I heard from some friends who knew her well. She was an excellent blues singer, and good at putting over her songs.'

Her childhood is completely undocumented, and it is not until she was in her mid-twenties that we have any knowledge of her. By 1918 she was a headline attraction on the T.O.B.A. circuit (Theatre Owners Booking Agency), and by 1921 she was filling the house at the Dream Theatre in Columbus, Georgia. Her life followed the general pattern of the women blues singers, and her journeys could be traced in the advertisements in contemporary local papers. She made appearances at the Lyric, New Orleans, the Bijou Theatre at Nashville and, by 1923, we find her at the Booker T. Washington Theatre in St Louis. In this same year she cut her first records for Columbia, *I've Got Everything A Good Woman Needs* and *Every Woman's Blues*. The performance of both these numbers is rather ponderous, and not helped by Fletcher Henderson's plodding and uninspired piano accompaniment; nor are the songs particularly interesting, but she does enough to prove that she had a good strong voice and a feeling for the blues. By October of this same year Clara had achieved quite a personal triumph, for she had recorded a couple of duets with Bessie Smith. Bessie's jealousy and contempt for other artists has already been mentioned, and that she consented to

CLARA SMITH
"The World's Champion Moaner"

EVERY blues thinks it's full of misery until Clara Smith goes to work on it. Blues, that no ordinary mortal dare tackle, subside into a melodious melody of moans and groans when Clara gets warmed up to her work.

Just look at her smile. What a sight for sore eyes! Listen to her voice. A balm for tired ears! You can hear her voice, and it seems like you can almost get the smile, too, on Columbia New Process Records.

Clara Smith is an Exclusive Columbia Artist

EASE IT . . . . PERCOLATIN' BLUES—*Piano Accompaniments by Lem Fowler*	14202-D	75c
YOU DON'T KNOW WHO'S SHAKIN' YOUR TREE—*Acc'p'd by Her Jazz Babies* CHEATIN' DADDY	14192-D	75c
GET ON BOARD—*Assisted by Sisters White and Wallace* . . . . LIVIN' HUMBLE—*Assisted by Sisters White and Wallace*	14183-D	75c
AIN'T NOTHIN' COOKIN' WHAT YOU'RE SMELLIN' . . . . SEPARATION BLUES	14160-D	75c

appear with her (and did so again in 1925) proves the respect this fiery woman held for Clara. It would be nice to record that these two blues, *Far Away Blues* and *I'm Going Back To My Use To Be*, were artistically satisfying, but this would be untrue. Once again it must be admitted that they were plodding, rather dreary songs, and Fletcher Henderson gives his usual depressing performance on the piano. Although he was constantly in work, his blues playing left a lot to be desired.

On April 10th, 1924, Clara recorded two excellent sides with Don Redman on clarinet and the ubiquitous Fletcher Henderson on piano. *War Horse*Mama and *Cold Weather Papa* show the immense strides this artist had made in a very short time. They are two slow blues songs of no startling originality, but she is able, with the help of Redman, to produce two attractive performances.

Seven days later she was back at Columbia with Henderson and Charlie Dixon on guitar to sing *West Indies Blues* and *Mean Papa Turn Your Key*. The former was far from easy to sing because of its suggestion of West Indian rhythms, which were becoming popular among the black people. According to Clyde Bernhardt, there were a considerable number of West Indian musicians in the various bands, although not all were anxious to admit this for some strange reason. Clara has no difficulty with the song and, of the recorded versions, this is by far the best. *Mean Papa Turn Your Key* is an extremely good song to which she does full justice. Clara is now well on the way to her peak and, from now

T.O.B.A. BOOKINGS

Liberty, Chattanooga, Tenn., Ma Rainey's "Paramount Flappers."

Bijou, Nashville, Tenn., Ida Cox "Raisin Cain" company.

Star, Shreveport, La., Byrd and Lockhart's "Vamp Man from Shanghai."

Houston, Tex., Chavers & Chavers, "Dusky Maids."

Gem, Hot Springs, Ark., Joe Carmouche's "Shake Your Feet."

Globe, Cleveland, Ohio, George Barton's "Roney Boy Sam."

Ogden, Columbus, Ohio, Doc Gardner's "Radio Ram the Melody Man."

Koppin, Detroit, Elmore Floyd's "Syncopated Sue."

Lincoln, Dallas, Tex., Sam Flashnick's "20 Dark Sports of Joy."

Pike, Mobile, Williams and Brown, "Happy Go Lucky."

Frolic, Birmingham, Ala., Sammie

Lewis' "Plantation Days."

Elmore, Pittsburgh, Pa., Irvin C. Miller's "Brown Skin Models."

Lincoln, Louisville, Billie Mack's "Pickings from Dixie."

Walker theater, Indianapolis, Ind., Clara Smith and company.

Palace, Dayton, Ohio, "Beans" and Susie and company.

Eighty-one theater, Atlanta, Ga., Mack and Green's "Sensational Sadie."

Douglas, Macon, Ga., Dusty Murray's "Chocolate Town."

Eagle and Palace, Ashville and Greensboro, N. C., Billy Pierson's "Miss Broadway."

Rex theater, Charlotte, N. C., Davenport and Smith's "Chicago Steppers."

Roosevelt, Cincinnati, Ohio, Whitman Sisters and their "Gang."

Washington, St. Louis, Mo., Bessie Smith's "Steamboat Days."

Jovland, Beaumont, Tex., and Palace, Lake Charles, La., Pearl

on, the improvement is marked. She is self-assured and very relaxed and there is no doubt of her stature.

Records followed at regular intervals, including some outstanding sessions with Louis Armstrong; *Nobody Knows How I Feel Dis Mornin'* and *Shipwrecked Blues* can be recommended if they can be found, but at the time of writing, they are extremely rare and have become collector's items.

Clara Smith's recordings are too numerous to be dealt with in a book of this length, but it is safe to say that most of the later discs are worth having in a collection. Among her best performances were *Salty Dog* and *My Brand New Papa*. *Salty Dog*, in particular, merits high praise. It always was a good song and Clara takes advantage of this; the result is an improvement on the celebrated Papa Charlie Jackson version with the Freddie Keppard orchestra. Even better, perhaps, was *Jelly Look What You Done Done*, with composer Porter Grainger on piano; this sexual blues comes over with a great impact and Miss Smith sings it with great relish. A most enjoyable experience for the listener.

In her mature years, she was undoubtedly a very good singer indeed. Bessie's voice was richer and more majestic, Clara's was more melodious and she was a little nearer to vaudeville, certainly in the early years, but as time went by she became more immersed in the blues tradition. At the very slowest tempos, no other singer could touch her, and she could and did, compete with the best.

By far the best description of Clara Smith was written many years ago by Carl van Vetchten in the magazine 'Vanity Fair' for March 1926. 'Her voice flutters agonizingly between tones. Music critics would say that she sings off key. What she really does, of course, is to sing quarter tones. She is billed as the "World's Greatest Moaner". She appears to be more of an artist than Bessie, but I suspect that this apparent artistry is spontaneous and uncalculated.

'As she comes upon the stage through folds of electric blue hangings at the back, she is wrapped in a black evening cloak

The shows listed in the Theatre Owner's Booking Agency column in The Chicago Defender *in March, 1929 included 'Ma' Rainey's 'Paramount Flappers', Ida Cox's 'Raisin' Cain', 'Cow Cow' Davenport and Iva Smith's 'Chicago Steppers', Bessie Smith's 'Steamboatin' Days' and the road shows of Butterbeans and Susie, and Clara Smith.*

bordered with white fur. She does not advance, but hesitates, turning her face in profile – Clara begins to sing;

> All day long I'm worried;
> All day long I'm blue;
> I'm so awfully lonesome,
> I doan know what to do.

> So I ask yo', Doctor,
> See if you can fin'
> Somethin' in yo' satchel
> To pacify my min'.

> Doctor! Doctor!

(Her tones become poignantly pathetic; tears roll down her cheeks)

> Write me a prescription fo' duh blues,
> De mean ole blues

(Her voice dies away in a mournful wail of pain, and she buries her head in the curtains.)

Clara Smith's tones uncannily take on the colour of the saxophone; again of the clarinet. Her voice is powerful or melancholy, by turns. It tears the blood from one's heart. One learns from her that the Negro's cry to a cruel cupid is as moving and elemental as his cry to God, as expressed in the spirituals.'

In 1935 at Detroit, Michigan, where she had been living in retirement, Clara Smith had a fatal heart attack, brought on no doubt from years of hard work touring the country in all types of shows. She died, like so many others, a forgotten woman.

Sippie Wallace, one of the best singers of the Classic era, is still living in Detroit in an ancient house which has a quite irresistible seedy elegance and old-world charm. A woman of quiet dignity and pleasing modesty, she was eager to talk of her career and her family. Sippie Thomas (her maiden name) comes from a genuine blues family. Her brother was Hersal Thomas, famous for his *Suitcase Blues*; Hersal recorded this when he was only fifteen years old – an amazing performance for one so young. Two other members of the Thomas family are well known to collectors. 'There was my elder brother, George Thomas,' said Miss Wallace, 'he played a bit, but he eventually became a music

Viva-tonal Recording

Columbia

ELECTRICAL PROCESS

Vocal
Trombone and
Piano accomp.

IT'S TIGHT LIKE THAT
(Dorsey and Whittaker
CLARA SMITH
14398-D
(147890)

MADE AND PAT'D IN U.S.A. JAN. 21,'13 AND RE. 16588, U.S.A. COLUMBIA PHONOGRAPH COMPANY, INC., NEW YORK

publisher and published two of my biggest hits, *Shorty George* and *Caldonia*, both my compositions, and you may remember *Up The Country*, and that was mine, too.'

The very fine pianist and singer, Hociel Thomas, was Sippie's niece. 'She died some years back, and I am taking care of her little girl. Hociel was a great singer, and played a mess of piano, *Go Down Sunshine* was one of her best known numbers, and she made a fine record of this in the 'forties. Papa Mutt Carey played some wonderful horn in the background. I am sorry to say my sister died a few months after making this.'

Sippie Wallace was born in Houston, Texas, at the turn of the century. November 1st, 1899, to be precise. Her childhood was spent in that town noted for its strong blues tradition. It was not until 1923 that she left for her first New York job. Then followed many years of touring, mostly on the T.O.B.A. circuit. Sippie did not mind the hard life on the road; singing and playing the piano was what she needed to do, so she was willing to put up with any hardship to achieve happiness. Her piano style is that rolling right-hand chordal style, with a solid left which is so typical of Texas. The pianists from this State are instantly recognisable. Her voice to this day remains rich and mellow.

Many blues enthusiasts have wondered how Sippie got her odd nickname; she explained: 'Well, it doesn't stand for Mississippi as a lot of folks think. You see, my sister kept teasing me because my teeth were so long in coming. I just had to sip my food all the time. So they naturally called me Sippie. My real name is Beulah, but I have not been called that for a long time. I guess most people have forgotten my Christian name.'

She had hidden herself away from everyone, living quietly with her husband, and many people thought her dead. Quite by chance Victoria Spivey ran across her when on a visit to her sister, Elton Spivey (the 'Za Zu Girl', who lives in Detroit). When Horst Lippmann's annual blues package tour was being compiled, Victoria mentioned her old friend to Willie Dixon, Lippmann's contact man in Chicago, and the rest was easy. Miss Wallace accepted the offer with some trepidation and set off for Europe, and a comeback. Those who heard her at the Royal Albert Hall, London, in 1966 had an unforgettable experience; superbly accompanied by Little Brother Mongomery, and almost scorning the microphone, her voice roared and leapt around this monument to Victorianism. She was the success of the show, and in every town she played, she received the same ecstatic reception. While in Europe, she also recorded an album, backed by Little Brother Montgomery and Roosevelt Sykes, in which she re-created her old and well-loved numbers. She had lost none of her old verve with the passing of the years. The records she made in the 'twenties are extremely difficult to obtain, and those with Armstrong are eagerly sought. It is fortunate that this album fills in the gap so adequately.

Now she is back in her Detroit home and the pace of her life has slackened. The church takes up much of her time, and she sings in the choir. Occasionally she does the local theatres when someone organises a blues concert. Sadly, the world passes her by in favour of the latest electronic discovery. The fans must think themselves lucky that they were able to hear the voice of Sippie Wallace, even if the Albert Hall was not exactly the most inspiring place for her. That night, she was way beyond its confines, back in some past age, singin' to the people.

Top: Sippie Wallace when she was making a hit record a month for the OKeh company. Little Brother Montgomery (above left) was friendly with Sippie's brother, Hersal Thomas, and nearly forty years later, accompanied her on a memorable European tour in 1966.

A Blues Mix

In her lifetime, Bertha 'Chippie' Hill made quite a reputation and there is no doubt she was very popular with the black audience to which she played. She was born in Charleston, South Carolina, in 1905, one of a family of sixteen. When she was quite a young girl (about thirteen) the family moved to New York to live with relatives; and it was in this Mecca of the New World that she first sang in public. Round about the time of the outbreak of the First World War, there was a famous night-spot called Leroy's to which all the talent found its way and it was here that the little girl obtained her first break. Ethel Waters was the star of Leroy's floor show, and very naturally the spot-light was focused on her. If Bertha didn't exactly steal the show from this already famous cabaret performer, she did well enough to prove her worth. Since she was only fourteen at the time, it must be admitted her feat was no mean one. She was so small that Leroy nicknamed her 'Chippie' and it stuck to her for the rest of her career.

It is quite possible that at this period 'Chippie' was a dancer only; the singing being added when she discovered that by this means she could earn extra dollars.

After some years around Harlem, she moved to Chicago. The great migration was in full swing and just after she arrived she won a talent and recording contest at the Coliseum on 16th and Wabash. Of this competition she said: 'A few of them [the contestants] were pretty good, but after I sang – that was all! I was about the biggest thing in Chicago that night.'

Her first session for OKeh on November 9th, 1925, with Louis Armstrong on cornet and Richard M. Jones, piano, produced two fine blues, *Low Land Blues* and *Kid Man Blues*. This was followed quickly by three more fine titles with the same people: *Lonesome All Alone Blues*, *Trouble In Mind* and the best of them, *Georgia Man*. Quite apart from 'Chippie's' fine contribution, the sides contain some wonderful examples of the Armstrong horn. What an inspiration Armstrong must have been to her; she was never to sing better. *Pratt City*, together with the aforementioned *Georgia Man*, are memorable performances.

King Oliver was in Chicago playing the Palladium dance hall where Bertha was singing. With Oliver and his music plus

Richard 'Myknee' Jones's eight-bar blues, Trouble in Mind, *was re-made by Bertha 'Chippie' Hill during her tragically brief come-back.*

'Chippie's' singing, the hall must have been one of the big attractions in the city. Naturally Bertha was not always working in town, she also had her share of touring, trudging wearily from one dreary one-night-stand to another, singing her blues throughout the country. She even had a few months with Ma Rainey and, like Bessie Smith before her, gained valuable experience.

In the late 'twenties, Bertha 'Chippie' Hill decided to quit the hard grind of show business and retire from the world of the blues, for she had married and naturally wanted a more settled life. For nearly twenty years she remained lost to us, but in 1946 she recorded some sides for Rudi Blesh's Circle label. Mr Blesh provided some fine musicians to back her: Lee Collins was on trumpet, Lovie Austin on piano and Baby Dodds on drums. On

73

some titles, Montana Taylor or Freddy Shayne replaced Miss Austin. *Around The Clock* and *Black Market Blues* can be recommended, if they can be found. In 1948 Bertha appeared at the Paris Jazz Festival and her success was sensational. Thus the middle-aged lady from Charleston made a come-back. Her future looked bright, and then Death walked out of the blue and claimed yet another victim. Death in the form of a hit-and-run driver. Poor 'Chippie' never had a chance. Terribly injured, she died in a Harlem hospital on Sunday, May 7th, 1950.

It would not be fair to say that she was the equal of Bessie Smith, she was not. On the tougher numbers like *Black Market Blues* she was in her element, but on the more subtle, melodic blues, she lacked a certain finesse. *How Long Blues* is almost a total failure. Bertha missed all the pathos and beauty of this Leroy Carr classic. Nevertheless, she will be remembered for such recordings as *Georgia Man*, *Pratt City Blues* and, of course, *Black Market*. These should be a suitable memorial for any singer.

As a blues centre, Texas has been almost as prolific as Mississippi. It has given the world some magnificent singers, guitarists and pianists. Not all of these were male. The Lone Star State has given us such great ladies as Moanin' Bernice Edwards, Lillian Glinn, Bessie Tucker, Victoria Spivey, Monette Moore, Mary Dixon, Sippie Wallace and Maggie Jones.

Most of the Texan women have that moaning quality in their voice – a style typified in Victoria Spivey or Lillian Glinn. It can be heard in Maggie Jones, who never achieved the fame of 'Chippie' Hill, but who was a far better singer. We know little of her background, a not unusual state of affairs, and one that points to the neglect with which these artists have been treated. It is believed that she was born about 1899, possibly in the northern part of the State, which is not too helpful, Texas then being the largest State in the Union. By the time she was twenty, she was performing in the East under her maiden name, Fae Barnes. In fact it was under this name that she made her first records. She was an attractive looking girl at that time, and photographs show a happy person with a most attractive smile. Paul Oliver has written: 'It is not clear whether she changed her name through marriage, or whether this was imposed by a recording company, for though her Black Swan and Paramount dates were under the name of Fae Barnes her coupling for Pathe/Perfect was as by Maggie Jones.' It was under the latter name that she made all

FAYE BARNES

Everybody who has heard the winsome Faye has predicted a wonderful future for her. No less a personage than Tony Langston, musical critic of the Chicago Defender, has praised her singing and has predicted a brilliant career for her. Faye Barnes is another new Paramount Blues star, formerly Black Swan star, and in just the few months that her records have been sold under the Paramount label, she has become one of the most popular artists in the catalog. Try one of her records and you will soon see why.

12099—**YOU DON'T KNOW MY MIND** Guitar Acc.   **Faye Barnes**
        GOODBYE BLUES Guitar Acc.   **Faye Barnes**

12136—**DO IT A LONG TIME PAPA** Piano Acc.   **Faye Barnes**
        I JUST WANT A DADDY Piano Acc.   **Faye Barnes**

her magnificent records for Columbia, thirty-four in all. VJM have produced an album of sixteen of these in chronological order. They show her to be a far better singer than some of equal fame, but her output was small compared to that of the Raineys and Smiths.

All her Columbia recordings were extremely good, apart from two with 'Alabama Joe', a pseudonym for the white Hawaiian guitarist, Roy Smeck, and even these contain a ghoulish humour (*Dangerous Blues* and *Suicide Blues*). Smeck's idea of how to accompany a singer such as Maggie is odd, to say the least. The lyrics of *Suicide Blues* strike a sombre note:

> If somebody find me when I'm dead and gone (*twice*)
> Say I did self murder, I died with my boots on.
>
> Took a Smith and Wesson and blew out my brains (*twice*)
> Didn't take no poison, couldn't stand the strain.

However, her masterpiece, and the song for which she will be remembered, is *Good Time Flat Blues* with a marvellous backing by Louis Armstrong. It tells the story of a woman running a 'good time flat,' until the police raid her. The beautiful melody was used later for the Storyville sequence in the film 'New Orleans' and re-titled *Farewell to Storyville*.

The most unusual blues she ever recorded is *North Bound Blues*, a bitter song dealing with conditions of the black people in the South. This kind of material, with its social comment, is rarely used by women singers, and it may well be the only example by a Classic Blues stylist.

> Goin' North, chile, where I can be free (*twice*)
> Where there's no hardship, like in Tennessee.
>
> Goin' where they don't have Jim Crow laws (*twice*)
> Don't have to work there like in Arkansas.

About 1930, she drifted into that unknown, lost land, where blues singers fade into obscurity, and nobody has been able to discover whether she is alive or dead. Thanks to the enterprise of the small private label, VJM, we can still enjoy her art.

We must now deal with some of the good artists who appeared on record during the decade when the Classic Blues were in full flower. It is to be regretted that the survey must be brief, but when the era was at its height so many women vocalists were being recorded that it would take several volumes to cover them adequately.

Martha Copeland was a singer who never achieved the fame she deserved, for at her finest, she could inject real blues feeling into her songs. Possessing a lovely full voice, she was at her very

MARTHA COPELAND

"Everybody's Mammy"

Well known and beloved by all other artists for her friendly disposition and generosity, Martha Copeland is appropriately called "Everybody's Mammy."

Martha is a great singer of blue. She always gives the best newest twist to each selection. This friendly star tours the country so frequently that she knows just the kind of music which will appeal to all. Then she records it for Columbia so that all may enjoy it whenever they wish.

Martha Copeland is an Exclusive Columbia Artist

SORROW VALLEY BLUES . . . . . }	14208-D	75c
SOUL AND BODY (He Belongs to Me) . . }		
THAT BLACK SNAKE MOAN . . . }	14196-D	75c
MINE'S JUST AS GOOD AS YOURS . . }		
ON DECORATION DAY (They'll Know Where to Bring Your Flowers to) . . }	14189-D	75c
FORTUNE TELLER BLUES . . . . }		
BLACK SNAKE BLUES . . . . . }	14161-D	75c
PAPA IF YOU CAN'T DO BETTER . . }		

Viva-tonal Recording. The Records without Scratch [11]

"ALBERTA—SING ME SOME BLUES!"

Who doesn't know this pretty little star who won such great success in her great stage play, "How Come?" Alberta's records are full of sentimental yearning. There is a depth of feeling in every note, and every word is clear as a bell. Alberta has won millions of friends with her pleading, plaintive Blues, and if she doesn't pull your heart strings, there's something wrong with you.

12001--DON'T PAN ME Vocal Blues. Orch. Acc.   **Alberta Hunter**
DADDY BLUES Vocal Solo, Orch. Acc.   **Alberta Hunter**

12005—DOWN HEARTED BLUES Comedy Solo, Orch. Acc.   **Alberta Hunter**
GONNA HAVE YOU AIN'T GONNA LEAVE YOU ALONE Comedy Solo. Orch. Acc.   **Alberta Hunter**

12006--I'M GOING AWAY JUST TO WEAR YOU OFF MY MIND Comedy Solo. Piano Acc.   **Alberta Hunter and Eubie Blake**
JAZZIN' BABY BLUES Comedy Solo, Piano Acc.   **Alberta Hunter and Eubie Blake**

12007—CRAZY BLUES Vocal Solo, Piano Acc.   **Sissel and Blake**
LONESOME MONDAY MORNING BLUES Comedy Solo, Orch. Acc.   **Alberta Hunter**

12008—YOU CAN'T HAVE IT ALL Comedy Solo, Orch. Acc.   **Alberta Hunter**
WHY DID YOU PICK ME UP WHEN I WAS DOWN, WHY DIDN'T YOU LET ME LAY Comedy Solo. Orch. Acc.   **Alberta Hunter**

⇢ ————————————————————— BLACK SWAN ———— ⇠
THE RACE'S OWN RECORD

best on that much recorded success by Victoria Spivey, *Black Snake Blues*. Cliff Jackson's fine piano accompaniment greatly helps to make this a most worthwhile disc. That she was popular with her own people is evident, for she made over thirty titles. That very good musician, trumpeter Louis Metcalf, can be heard behind her on *Soul And Body* and *Sorrow Valley Blues*. The four sides on RCA which were issued in Great Britain, *When*

The Wind Makes Connection With Your Dry Goods, Stole My Man Blues, Hard Hearted Mama and *I Don't Care Who Ain't Got Nobody*, do her less than justice, being rather feeble music-hall songs for the most part.

Very different in style is Alberta Hunter, one of the earliest of the women singers to record. Alberta has a sweet, pure voice, not really suited to the blues, but being such a good artist, she can at times produce a good blues disc. *Down Hearted Blues* was her first success as far back as 1922, and until Bessie Smith came along and deliberately carved her up with the same song, Miss Hunter's version was considered to be the best.

Alberta Hunter was born in Memphis, Tennessee, but her travels have taken her all over the world. Like Edith Wilson, she looks upon herself as an all-round performer rather than a blues singer, and of course, this is a correct estimation. She is known to have recorded under the pseudonym of Josephine Beatty, for contractual reasons, no doubt. However, nothing very startling came from any of the Beatty dates. All through the slump Alberta was in work, such was her versatility. In 1939 she co-starred with Ethel Waters in the Broadway musical, Mamba's Daughter. The Second World War saw her travelling all over the world entertaining the troops; for this work she was decorated. She is now a nurse at the Goldwater Memorial Hospital on Welfare Island and has given up singing and acting. However, Victoria

Left: Alberta Hunter popularised a diluted form of the Classic blues. Sara Martin (below left) was dramatic on stage but less so on record while Lizzie Miles (below right) sang vaudeville songs in the 'twenties.

Above: in later years, Lizzie Miles specialised in Creole songs.

Spivey did persuade her to make some titles for Prestige. Of these the best were *I Got Myself A Working Man* and *Got A Mind To Ramble*.

A singer who made a very big reputation throughout the 'twenties was Sara Martin, yet she was never a really great blues singer. The records she made varied considerably, on many she sounded stilted and very unrelaxed. The influence of the vaudeville stage comes through strongly at times, and some of her material is rather poor. Occasionally, she did hit a groove and when this happened, she could be quite pleasing, as on her very original *Brother Ben*. She was born in Louisville, but little more is known of her. To dismiss Miss Martin in a few brief lines may seem unfair, but so many of her records are dull and uninspiring. The sides she did with King Oliver can be recommended, particularly *Death Sting Me Blues*. On stage she was a fine showwoman and held her audience in the palm of her hand. Unfortunately, she was unable to put this across on record.

New Orleans, strangely enough, has never been celebrated for blues singers; such men as Lonnie Johnson and Pleasant Joe were the exceptions. One of the few women singers born in the Crescent city, in 1895, was Lizzie Miles, a large woman with an equally large voice. Her repertoire was fantastically wide, including everything from vaudeville ballads, Creole songs (sung in

Creole French) to the more earthy type of blues. These latter she shouted out with vim and vigour. That she would not be placed among the immortals may be true, but at her best she was a most formidable singer. She died on March 17th, 1963.

It would not be unfair to say that Trixie Smith's big reputation among collectors is based on the result of two sessions in the recording studios. The Armstrong set in 1925 which included *The World's Jazz Crazy And So Am I* and *Railroad Man Blues*, and the Charlie Shavers/Sidney Bechet session in 1938 which produced, among other great songs, *Freight Train Blues*. This is no derogatory statement, for Trixie was an exceedingly good singer, who owed a big debt to vaudeville, but on the dates in question, everything was completely right, members of the band were obviously feeling in the mood for jazz, and the atmosphere in the studios must have been conducive to good playing. The result was an intriguing blend of voice and instruments. She was lucky to find conditions so ideal. Possibly if Sara Martin had had her luck, she, too, might have been remembered with the same respect. Trixie Smith died in 1943.

For only a comparatively short period of her very long career could Ethel Waters be classed as a Classic Blues singer. She is, however, one of the most versatile entertainers, and, with the

With her eyes full of tears Trixie Smith sobs—"I hate to hear that engine blow O-O-OO-OO. She can't ride on the freight train—mean cruel brakeman won't even let her ride the blind. So the whistle blows—the train goes—and Trixie goes to her room and hides. But when a man gets the Blues, he gets on a freight train and rides.

2211 { Freight Train Blues— { Don't Shake It No More   Trixie Smith and Her Down Home Syncopators

late Florence Mills, ranks among the greatest of her race. In her early years – and these are the only ones that concern us – she had a most flexible voice, sometimes with a hoarse croak which she used to great advantage. In the early 'twenties she recorded a series of very fine blues and blues-based songs such as *Tell 'Em About Me, Back Bitin' Mama, Go Back Where You Stayed Last Night, Shake That Thing* and *Bring Me Your Greenbacks*. Gradually over the years her activities broadened, and she became a fine actress on both stage and screen: her performance in Member Of The Wedding won high praise from the New York critics, and will be remembered by many readers, for she repeated it in the screen version. She continued to record, and although many discs were very good, they do not come within the scope of this book. She has now retired, but is very active with Billy Graham. It is interesting to speculate on just how many of the thousands of people who have attended Graham's meetings realise that the dignified old lady with the rather shaky voice was once one of America's brightest stars.

ETHEL WATERS

"America's Foremost Ebony Comedienne"

GLANCE at Ethel Waters, and you will understand why this Race star is hailed as "America's Foremost Ebony Comedienne." Miss Waters is something more than a singer, something more than an actress — she is one of the greatest artists, in the musical sense, that the Race has yet produced.

Everybody, old and young, white folks as well as Race, flock to the theatre where Miss Waters is appearing. And everybody buys, plays, and loves her records.

Ethel Waters is an Exclusive Columbia Artist

The Lesser-Known Singers

We have now met all the leading members of the cast, but the show is by no means ready for the stage. What of the supporting players? Those whose talent (in most cases) is great, but for some reason or other has not won them stardom. At the height of the boom, literally hundreds of women were recorded by all sorts of people for all types of companies, all hoping to get the Big Hit which would rocket them to the pinnacle of success. Many of these ladies were unspeakably bad, and in some cases it is a complete mystery how anyone could have thought them good enough to record at all, far less reach the top of the tree! However, many others were very good indeed. Much too good to be dismissed in a few lines. Unfortunately, it is not possible to deal with more than a fraction of the whole. The list, therefore, must be selective and rather personal.

The voice of Ada Brown was full, rich and very mellow. It had that vibrant quality which distinguishes artists. Yet she seldom recorded. When the craze for female singers was at its height, Ada cut hardly anything. Her first session was with the Benny Moten band as far back as September 1923, when she made *Ill Natured Blues*, *Break O'Day Blues* and, perhaps the best of all, *Evil Mama Blues*. *Ill Natured Blues* and *Break O' Day* are vaudeville based numbers, but Ada injects real blues feeling into both of them. The band, like all the famous Kansas City groups of the period, knows just how to play blues, with the result that the songs sound better than they really are. *Evil Mama* is much closer to the genuine article, and must rate among the best of Miss Brown's small output.

Not until almost three years later did she return to the studio. On March 10th, 1926, she recorded two excellent songs: *Panama Limited Blues* and *Tia Juana Man*. The accompanying band was again ideal for this material, consisting of George Mitchell, cornet, Albert Nicholas, clarinet and alto, Barney Bigard, tenor, Luis Russell, piano, and Johnny St Cyr, banjo. Only two titles were cut, but both of them were splendid examples of Classic Blues singing. *Panama Limited* has the rather hackneyed theme of the train taking her good man away, but Ada manages to make it a very personal affair. She sings with great strength and vigour, and one can believe that she is really suffering all the emotions of a deserted woman. This is singing worthy of the highest praise. *Tia Juana Man* has what Jelly Roll Morton has called the 'Spanish tinge', and it is a difficult song to put across, but Miss Brown acquits herself splendidly. Both songs are notable for good melodic solos from George Mitchell. The recording, too, is excellent, and Ada's voice comes through strongly.

Ada Brown, like other women singers, was billed as 'The Queen of the Blues'. She teamed with 'Bojangles' Robinson in the Broadway hit Brown Buddies, *but died forgotten in 1950.*

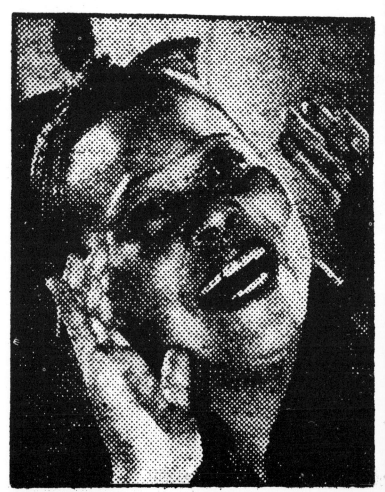

One more session in May of this same year with Porter Grainger on piano almost completes her career. In the 'forties she appeared with Fats in the film 'Stormy Weather'. In this she sang a duet with the irresistible Mr Waller, *That Ain't Right*. This amusing if slight little song was issued for the American Forces on V-Disc. After this picture we hear no more of Ada Brown. She made no more records, and what happened to her is a mystery. It is quite incomprehensible that an artist of her quality should be so neglected. Perhaps she lacked the ability to push herself before the right people, such as recording managers and film producers. Who can tell? Whatever the reason, Ada Brown remained until her death, some years ago, one of the forgotten ladies of the blues.

Few collectors will have heard of the delightful and talented Miss Eliza Brown (or Liza, both have been used on the Columbia label). Her duets with Ann Johnson – another extremely good, but unknown singer – *Get On Out Of Here* and *Let's Get It Straight* are both charming and amusing little cameos. Jim Jackson adds to the fun, putting in some wry comments and backchat. It is all typical of the hokum the coloured acts offered in the music halls and on record. The famous Butterbeans and Susie were possibly the supreme performers in this style but there is little on any modern label to represent this important period of Negro vaudeville.

Eliza Brown, like her namesake, Ada, recorded very few titles, and while she may have lacked the strength of this fine singer, she did have a most attractive voice. *Peddlin' Man* and *If Papa Has Outside Lovin'*, with Wesley Wilson on piano and backchatting Eliza, are very much in the style of the duets with Ann Johnson. There is a wonderful atmosphere about these sides, and the humour is most captivating. A good cornet player can be heard on both sides (apart from a horrible fluff in the introduction to *Outside Lovin'*) who sounds very like Deamus Dean.

Even more modest is the recording career of Hattie Burleson, about whom nothing is known. She sounds as if she might belong to that group of Texas singers previously mentioned (*see* page 74). Both the tonal quality of her voice, and the ability to convey, without exactly doing so, the moan, so common among Texan women (Moanin' Bernice Edwards and Victoria Spivey, for example), all point to her coming from that region. Furthermore, one of her only known recording sessions, in November 1928, took place in Dallas, Texas, and one of the songs she sang on the date was *Jim Nappy*, a favourite of the Texas blues pianists. As if to clinch matters, Miss Burleson is known to have associated with such Texas bluesmen as Buster Pickens and his friends. Perhaps the best and most original blues on this session was *Sadie's Servant Room Blues*, a little song about class distinction and the thoughts of a black servant girl working in a white household. The song must have appealed to many of her listeners in similar circumstances. On a superficial level, the blues is just a rather charming little song about a serving maid, but underneath lies a shrewd piece of social comment.

The reverse is a blues of another kind. This time dealing with credulity, *Superstitious Blues*. While not quite as good, it has some good lyrics and is beautifully sung by Hattie. *Jim Nappy* and its backing, *Bye Bye Baby*, complete the set. *Jim Nappy* is equal to any of the versions sung and played by the Texas Barrelhouse pianists. *Bye Bye Baby* is less original, but just as well sung as the other three. The band that accompanies her contains that fine and rather under-rated trumpeter, Don Albert. Albert is still active, and lives in San Antonio in Texas. Unfortunately he gets little opportunity to record.

Mary Dixon is yet another singer who was born in Texas. Victoria Spivey knew and admired her singing. It would appear that during the years 1928–29 she spent some time in New York, for all her ten titles, the result of five recording sessions, were cut in that city. The first of these was on Monday, July 30th, 1928, for Vocalion, and the last on Thursday, October 3rd, 1929, for Columbia. On Saturday, August 24th, 1929, with Louis Metcalf playing some fine trumpet in the background, she cut her two best sides, *Black Dog Blues* and *Fire And Thunder Blues*. *Black Dog* is a blues about another girl going to steal the singer's man, with use of the animal symbol, so popular among bluesmen (and women). *Fire And Thunder* has a storm motive and contains some fine lyrics:

> If I must die, I'd rather die on land, (*twice*)
> Than to be buried under all this mud and sand.

On *Black Dog*, Mary indulged in some moaning and growling which heightens the tension greatly. Altogether a very satisfying record.

Lillian Glinn is a much smoother singer who aims at a more sophisticated urban audience. Nevertheless, there are overtones of the country blues, and she is a very good artist with a personal

Lillian Glinn's recordings were made on location in her home city of Dallas, Texas, and on tour in Atlanta and New Orleans.

style. Her best known titles are *Shreveport Blues, Black Man Blues, Atlanta Blues* and *All The Week Blues.* All have been re-issued on an EP and this disc makes a good representative collection of her work. Undoubtedly her best recording is the really superb *Shake It Down,* re-issued on the two-volume set which was produced as a companion to Paul Oliver's book *The Story of The Blues.* Here she swings into a medium tempo blues and

Overleaf: veterans of the stage and road shows at a Spivey recording session in 1962. Left to right: blues singer Hannah Sylvester, entertainer Pat Blackman, Victoria Spivey, her daughter Jackie Lynn Wilson who toured with the shows as a child singer, and Lucille Hegamin.

Above: Cleo Gibson's only record was made by a field unit in Atlanta.

comes close to stealing a side which contains some magnificent material, including tracks by Bessie Smith and Butterbeans and Susie.

One of the great mysteries surrounding the Classic singers is Cleo Gibson. Who was she? Her full name was Cleothus Gibson, and she was a member of the team of Gibson and Gibson, a vaudeville duo, presumably on the lines of Butterbeans and Susie, Coot Grant and Wesley 'Sox' Wilson. How did she obtain a recording date? Presumably because of her amazing resemblance to Bessie Smith; and why after making only two songs was she allowed to disappear? One must assume that it was this almost uncanny likeness to Miss Smith that made and killed her off at one and the same time. Miss Gibson sang a sexual blues *I've Got Ford Movements In My Hips* and *Nothing But The Blues*, backed by Henry Mason on trumpet, J. Neal Montgomery on piano and an unknown guitar. There is little need to comment on this fine disc. Miss Gibson has not quite the power and strength of Bessie at her best, but she fooled a number of critics and collectors when the record first appeared. It is tempting to write much more about Cleo Gibson and the mystery that embraces her. If only she had returned to the recording studios after the death of the woman she admired so much, she might have gone on from where Bessie Smith left off, instead of being just an intriguing name on a record label.

In complete contrast are Edmonia and Katherine Henderson, both of whom lean heavily on the vaudeville fence, but both these ladies have made interesting discs. *Brown Skin Man* and *Traveling Blues* are very good examples of Edmonia's style, with beautiful accompaniment by Lovie Austin and her Blues Seren-

EDMONIA HENDERSON
"The Melodious Blues Singer"

Edmonia is an old-time stage favorite, who has been in big-time vaudeville for years. She recently won the Paramount Blues Singer Contest. Edmonia leaped into fame with her famous song, "Brown-Skin Man"—a song that will never grow old and that is selling faster and faster every month. Edmonia has an exclusive, clever melodious way of warbling her Blues—the kind that will make you forget work and trouble, and will make you want to listen to more. Put your money on Edmonia. You will never be sorry.

12203—HATEFUL BLUES Acc. Lovie Austin and Her Blues Serenaders
Edmonia Henderson

MAMA DON'T WANT SWEET MAN ANY MORE Acc. Lovie Austin and Her Blues Serenaders
Edmonia Henderson

12097—IF YOU SHEIK ON YOUR MAMA Acc. Lovie Austin and Her Blues Serenaders
Edmonia Henderson

MEAN PAPA TURN IN YOUR KEY Acc. Lovie Austin and Her Blues Serenaders
Ida Cox

12095—BROWN SKIN MAN Acc. Lovie Austin and Her Serenaders
Edmonia Henderson

TRAVELING BLUES Acc. Lovie Austin and Her Serenaders
Edmonia Henderson

12084—BLACK MAN BLUES Acc. Lovie Austin and Her Blues Serenaders
Edmonia Henderson

WORRIED 'BOUT HIM BLUES Acc. Lovie Austin and Her Blues Serenaders
Edmonia Henderson

aders, together with Tommy Ladnier and Jimmy O'Bryant, all playing superbly. It is worthy of note that *Brown Skin Man* was the record that made Edmonia Henderson's name. Ladnier plays particularly well on this. *Mama Don't Want A Sweet Man Anymore* is a similar type of song. Once again it can be classed as a music hall blues ballad, but if for nothing else (and there is a lot in its favour) the disc would be worthwhile for Tommy Ladnier, who plays most sensitive horn throughout. Mention must be made of her two titles with Jelly Roll Morton, *Dead Man Blues* and *Georgia Grind*: both are excellent, and Morton's accompaniments are beyond praise.

Katherine Henderson's chief claim to fame was that she was a niece of Fletcher Henderson. Apart from the fact that she recorded a vocal version of Louis Armstrong's great success, *West End Blues*, she has little to recommend her to readers of this book. Her voice was over-sweet, and she put her material across in a rather lachrymose manner. There was more than a suspicion of ham (one of the bad elements in the cheaper class of vaudeville artist) in her presentation. The false note of sentimentality and the rather sickly voice marred what talent she may have had.

A much better artist was Virginia Liston, whose choice of material was extremely good. *Rolls Royce Papa* and *I'm Gonna Get A Man That's All* contain good, forthright singing. Miss Liston cut her first records on September 14th, 1923 and her last on May 26th, 1926. Between those dates she made a number of items of considerable interest.

Margaret Johnson was another sweet-voiced singer, but without the cloying sentimentality of Katherine Henderson. Apart from

Below: an advertisement for a Margaret Johnson record. Right: Virginia Liston, whose home in Washington was 'open house' to blues singers.

being issued by the OKeh company in the United States, two of her records were issued in Britain on the old Parlophone red label, *If I Let You Get Away With It* and *E Flat Blues* with *Nobody Knows The Way I Feel This Mornin'* and *Absent Minded Blues*. Both are rare items prized by collectors, mainly for the superb accompaniments. On the former two titles, Sidney Bechet plays magnificently.

Mary Mack was the second half of a vaudeville act similar to Butterbeans and Susie, and for many years Billy & Mary Mack were popular stars. She made a few discs on her own, and proved to be a good singer in the Classic Blues idiom. *Stingaree Man* and *I Vouch For My Man* are perhaps the best. Although recorded in 1937, when the Classic period had faded, this was one of the carry-overs from that great era. The Macks are still alive and living quietly in Chicago, where Mary runs a profitable dress-making business. They occasionally re-create their act for various charities. A gentle, kindly couple, they are still very interested in music.

Viola McCoy cannot be dismissed in one short paragraph, yet we have little space to do this fine singer justice. She belongs to the great vaudeville tradition, but in all she does there is a strong jazz strain. She was, to use a modernism, a real swinger, and when she got into a groove she was a grand performer. Possessing a lovely contralto voice and fine diction, she was able to project herself through even the worst recording. An example of what she could do with a poor song is her version of *Laughin' Cryin' Blues*, a dreadful 'novelty' number. Miss McCoy somehow manages to make the awful lyrics bearable, and even her laugh in the middle section comes off, it is so perfectly timed.

Her masterpiece, however, is *If Your Good Man Quits You, Don't Wear No Black*, a fast blues romp accompanied by members of the Fletcher Henderson Orchestra. The band plays with immense verve and vigour, and Viola is in top form. The reverse, *I Ain't Gonna Marry, Ain't Gonna Settle Down*, is taken at a slower tempo, but is almost the equal of *If Your Good Man Quits You*. This 1927 recording remains a minor masterpiece to this day. It would be true to say that in the three years she was recording most prolifically she hardly ever made a bad record.

Mattie Hite, according to Frankie 'Half Pint' Jackson, was a long, tall woman, who flavoured her act with some extremely risqué songs, but she could sing good blues when she liked. She

Right: Viola McCoy early in her career as a singer.

Above: Hannah Sylvester in retirement.

was best known for a very fine version of *St James' Infirmary*. The backing, *Texas Twist*, is also worth hearing.

Lastly in this brief survey, we come to Hannah Sylvester, a rock of a woman, and a singer of tough, raw blues. Her early work is extremely hard to find, and she did not make many records. *Pappa – Better Watch Your Step* and *Gulf Coast Blues* are representative. In the 'sixties she was discovered by Victoria Spivey and she cut some superb titles for her label, *Mr Cab* and *Big Black Limousine* being quite outstanding.

There are of course, many more singers worthy of note, many, too, who can safely be ignored. The list is almost endless, but those mentioned in this chapter are the main and most important of the less-known singers. It is up to the reader to discover the rest for himself. It will take years, but, once he acquires a taste for the Classic Blues, he will enjoy his search.

Conclusion:
The Post~Classic Period

So a whole era passed into history sadly undocumented, and the women who created it retired or died. Only Ma Rainey, Bessie Smith and the still very active Victoria Spivey are remembered. The others, let us call them the 'splinter group', who sang blues, ballads and popular songs of the day, and who were one, or even two steps away from the rural blues, but ironically were responsible for the scene as we know it, faded and disappeared. It is a

'Ma' Rainey died in 1939 but is still warmly remembered.

pity, for as this book has tried to show, the vaudeville singers had great talent and no little charm. Furthermore, as we have seen, vaudeville played an important part in the basic style. The term Classic Blues has always been a very inaccurate description for such a varied form. However we twist and turn the phrase, we come back to the strongest influence, that of vaudeville and the music hall. It is in every so-called Classic Blues singer, from Lucille Hegamin to Bessie Smith; stronger in some than in others, but inescapable. It would be more correct to call them Vaudeville Blues. Unfortunately, vaudeville is a dirty word in these days of talentless pop stars, so for better or worse, Classic Blues remains to cover a variety of related styles.

It was, of course, inevitable that the sweet-voiced ladies should pass into obscurity, for while Ma Rainey, Bessie Smith and others of that calibre were preaching in song a universal and timeless message that came from the very root of the blues, the more refined and sophisticated artists – for the time – were very much of the period. What they sang was relevant to the Roaring 'Twenties. They spoke to the people through light-hearted song (the coloured population, mainly), and employed an idiom that was part of the world as it appeared then. So the people took them to their hearts, and brought them into their homes by way of the gramophone record.

Soon everyone was to be stunned and crushed by the financial

Below left: Rosetta Howard, who sang with the Harlem Hamfats. Below right and opposite: Lil Green. She made many good blues but her hit record was Romance in the Dark.

crisis of 1929 and 1930. The stars' working lives were brought to a sudden end. The world was changing, and in the 'thirties was rushing towards inevitable disaster. In the mid- and late-'thirties, there was a temporary improvement: the calm before the storm. Small pockets of resistance appeared and some good singers could be heard. Bessie Smith's cousin, Ruby Smith, was singing quite well, and was proving popular. Rosetta Crawford cut some sides which included Tommy Ladnier and Mezz Mezzrow and were much admired: *I'm Tired Of Fattening Frogs For Snakes* and *My Man Jumped Salty On Me*. Rosetta Howard also made a name for herself singing with an excellent little blues band led by the McCoy brothers (Charlie and Joe), and on her own she recorded *Rosetta Blues* and *If You're A Viper*, the latter a humorous song about pot smoking.

In this post-classic period, one of the finest singers to emerge was the late Lil Green, who was recording for Victor/Bluebird right up to America's entry into the War. She made some extremely good blues and blues ballads, and was usually accompanied by Big Bill Broonzy (who also wrote some of her material)

and her regular pianist, Simeon Henry. Such blues as *Mr Jackson From Jacksonville*, *Now What Do You Think* and *Blow Top Blues* – the latter with a large swing orchestra – can be strongly recommended. The theme of madness and the fear of being taken to Bellevue comes through with dramatic intensity. The agitated brass figures (very reminiscent of Don Redman's scoring, who may be responsible for both the band and the arrangement), emphasize the agony of the singer who is on the brink of madness. This blues was one of the great Dinah Washington successes, but Miss Green's version is superior in every way. Lil had a nasal, rather high-pitched voice which she used to great advantage, and she became a popular artist during her brief career. *Why Don't You Do Right*, which she wrote, was one of the songs that put Peggy Lee on the road to fame.

Viola Wells, better known as Miss Rhapsody, is a singer with a shining talent, but unfortunately is little known to the young collector. Among musicians, however, she has always been a favourite. The late Jimmy Lunceford said she was the greatest singer since Bessie Smith. While Benny Carter, no mean judge, stated publicly that 'Miss Rhapsody is the greatest blues singer in the country'.

This startlingly beautiful woman has been a professional singer all her life, although she is devoting much of her time to the Church at the present time, and seldom works professionally. At the peak of her career she sang with all the finest musicians, and now, at sixty-eight, can look back on her life with satisfaction.

The series of sides she made for Savoy in 1944 and 1945 were all excellent and the various sessions featured some of the cream of the jazz world in the small accompanying groups. Such men as Frankie Newton, Emmett Berry and Freddy Webster on trumpet, Lockjaw Davis or Walter 'Foots' Thomas on tenor and Cozy Cole on drums were to be heard. She recorded four very good titles for the Spivey label, of which only one has been issued, *See See Rider*, and it is to be hoped that the other three will appear in due course. In particular *Tall, Tan And Terrific*, a fine, swinging blues helped along by some good drumming by Sonny Greer. Miss Wells also did a test session for CBS, which included both blues and popular numbers, plus a Spiritual to add variety. These

Left: Viola Wells with Victoria Spivey. Below: The Apollo Theatre, Harlem, where many of the 'post-Classic' women singers worked.

have never been issued, and at this late date it seems unlikely that they ever will be. A great pity, for her singing on every number is quite marvellous and should be brought to the notice of the discriminating collector. Viola Wells is not unhappy with the situation, she is a contented woman who has lived a full life, and most important for her, she has the admiration of the jazz musicians.

The Second World War struck yet another blow at the ailing Classic Blues. By the time the uneasy peace came, the past belonged to an almost different planet. These artists could not possibly appeal to a young generation brought up on Rock 'n' Roll. However, the evergreen Miss Spivey was not to be silenced, and the veteran singers she gathered around her were able to create some interest in the older tradition, while her own songs always kept up to date and could strike a response in the young.

Today, Spivey apart, it does not look too good. Occasionally a new singer does appear who seems to have understood the style, and to have modernised it slightly. One such is Jeanne Carroll, who works with the Franz Jackson band. She has also recorded for Little Brother Montgomery. To hear her rich voice swelling out above Brother's piano on *Oh Daddy* and *Vicksburg Blues* is to experience a sensation of *déjà vu*, perhaps, but Miss Carroll knows she is in the royal tradition of the blues queens; a tiny hope in a vast desert of emptiness, as far as the female blues is concerned.

Our knowledge of this portion of blues history is still sparse, and this is to be regretted for, quite apart from the music they made, these women have a story to tell of the early days, of the Tent and Minstrel shows where so many jazzmen 'paid their dues'. They know all about the circuses and the men who played in the bands, they can tell us more about the famous T.O.B.A. circuit – in fact, they can fill in so many gaps, but nobody seems to care. The story of jazz and the blues is incomplete. Surely someone will start an investigation before it is too late. What Mamie Smith set in motion so many years ago with her *Crazy Blues* must not be allowed to wither, certainly not until a thorough investigation has been conducted. Mamie may have sung about craziness, but that is no reason why we should become crazy too. Time is running out, the Classic Blues may be over, but some of the old ladies remain. They should be contacted and recognised for the great artists they have always been. Alas, we forget so easily.

Right: Jeanne Carroll, a young singer who works in the Classic idiom.

Acknowledgments

I am greatly indebted to Paul Oliver for the loan of his files and tapes, which proved to be invaluable. To Bill Daynes-Wood, I owe more than I can say. He did much of the hard, boring work such as transcribing tapes. Brian Knight was of great assistance in very many ways, and his data were a blessing.

My grateful thanks to Victoria Spivey and Leonard Kunstadt for their immense help at all times. And I raise my hat to Lennie's magazine, 'Record Research', which filled in a lot of gaps.

The musicians and singers gave generously of their time to advise me, and I am especially indebted to blues singer and trombonist, Clyde Bernhardt, ex Fats Waller reedman, Rudy Powell, and blues singer and pianist, Little Brother Montgomery. I do not know what I would have done without the help of Mrs Peggy Webb and Derek and Lorna Bown, who between them typed out the final draft, and to whom I am extremely grateful.

Finally we come to the one who suffered all my fits of depression and bad temper when things got a bit out of hand, who corrected my awful spelling, checked up on many details, and who at all times was ready to calm me down; for my wife, Mary, the words 'Thank you' are entirely inadequate.

Book List

As this is the only book devoted to the Classic Blues, the literature on the subject is scarce. The following are the works that do have something to say about the subject and the singers, but sometimes the mention is brief.

BRADFORD, Perry, *Born With The Blues*. Oak Publications, New York, 1965.

DIXON, Robert M. W., and GODRICH, John, *Blues and Gospel Records 1902 to 1942*. Storyville Publications & Co., London, 1969 (revised edition). Contains full discographical details of classic blues recordings.

CHARTERS, Samuel B., and KUNSTADT, Leonard, *Jazz – The History of the New York Scene*. Doubleday & Co. Inc., New York, 1962.

JONES, LeRoi, *Blues People*. MacGibbon & Kee Ltd., London, 1965: Jazz Book Club, London, 1966.

McCARTHY (editor), Albert, *Jazz on Record*. Hanover Books, London, 1968: Oak Publications, New York, 1969.

OLIVER, Paul, *Bessie Smith*. Cassell & Co. Ltd., London, 1960.

OLIVER, Paul, *Blues Fell This Morning*. Cassell & Co. Ltd., London, 1960: Horizon Books, New York, 1962.

OLIVER, Paul, *Conversation With The Blues*. Cassell & Co. Ltd., London, 1965: Horizon Books, New York, 1966.

OLIVER, Paul, *Screening The Blues*. Cassell & Co. Ltd., London, 1968: Oak Publications, New York, 1970.

OLIVER, Paul, *The Story of The Blues*. Barrie & Jenkins, London, 1969: Chilton Book Company, Philadelphia, Pa., 1969.

SHAPIRO, N., and HENTOFF, N., *Hear Me Talkin' To Ya*. Peter Davies Ltd., London, 1955: Chilton Book Company, Philadelphia, Pa., 1969.

STEARNS, Marshall, *The Story of Jazz*. Oxford University Press, New York, 1956: Sidgwick & Jackson Ltd., London, 1957: Mentor Press, New York, 1958.

WATERS, Ethel, *His Eye is on The Sparrow*. W. H. Allen & Co., London, 1951.

Jazz Journal, *Storyville*, and *Jazz Monthly* print articles on blues and sometimes deal with women singers in general.

Blues Unlimited and *Blues World* are magazines devoted to the blues, but seldom carry much on female singers.

Discography

Although there has been a general lack of interest and respect for many Classic Blues singers, a considerable number of re-issues have been made available from time to time; these have been issued mainly for the accompanying groups usually consisting of star players. This has unfortunately led to a lot of below-average singers being re-issued but the following, however, can be recommended as being representative. Some are unavoidably on rare 78's and will only be obtainable with considerable difficulty. Nevertheless for the sake of completeness the discs have been included. Wherever possible the numbers of microgroove re-issues are given.

Abbreviations

The following abbreviations are used in this list. Labels are American unless country of origin is indicated below.

A of H	Ace of Hearts (England)	OK	OKeh
Aud	Audubon	Par	Parlophone (England)
BB	Bluebird	Phi	Philips (England)
Br	Brunswick	Pm	Paramount
CBS	CBS (England)	Pres	Prestige
Cam	Cameo	QRS	QRS
Cir	Circle	RCA	RCA Victor (England)
Co	Columbia	RBF	RBF
De	Decca	Riv	Riverside
Em	Emerson	Sav	Savoy
Font	Fontana	Spi	Spivey
F.M.	F.M.	Stor	Storyville (England)
Ge	Gennett	Swa	Swaggie (Australia)
Hist	Historical	Vi	Victor
J.S.	Jazz Society (France)	VJM	VJM (England)
Maj	Majestic	Vo	Vocalion
Mil	Milestone	Xtra	Xtra (England)

Artist's name	Title	Original release	Microgroove re-issue
BROWN, Ada	Ill Natured Blues	OK 8123	
	Break o' Day Blues	OK 8101	
	Evil Mama Blues	—	
	Panama Limited Blues	Vo 1009	
	Tia Juana Man	—	
BROWN, Eliza	Get On Out Of Here	Co 14466	CBS 66232
	Let's Get It Straight	—	
	Peddlin' Man	Co 14471	
	If Papa has Outside Lovin'	—	
BURLESON, Hattie	Bye Bye Baby	Br 7054	
	Jim Nappy	—	
	Sadie's Servant Room Blues	Br 7042	Hist ASC5829–16
CARROLL, Jeanne	Oh Daddy		F.M. 1001
	Vicksburg Blues	—	
COPELAND, Martha	Black Snake Blues	Co 14161	
	Soul and Body (He Belongs to Me)	Co 14208	
	Sorrow Valley Blues	—	
	When The Wind Makes Connection With Your Dry Goods	Vi 20548	RCA 7183

Artist's name	Title	Original release	Microgroove re-issue
	Stole My Man Blues	Vi 20769	—
	Hard Hearted Mama	Vi 20548	—
	I Don't Care Who Ain't Got Nobody	Vi 20769	—
	Desert Blues	Co 14352	CBS 66232
COX, Ida	*Coffin Blues*	Pm 12318	Riv RLP1019
	Mean Papa Turn Your Key	Pm 12097	—
	Bone Orchard Blues	Pm 12664	Riv RLP1007
	Wild Women Don't Get The Blues	Pm 12228	—
	Fogyism	Pm 12690	—
	Western Union Blues	Pm 12664	—
	Tree Top Tall Papa	Pm 12690	—
	Death Letter Blues	Vo 05336	
	Hard Time Blues	Vo 05298	
	Last Mile Blues	OK 6405	
	I Can't Quit That Man	—	
	Blues for Rampart Street		Riv RLP374
CRAWFORD, Rosetta	*I'm Tired Of Fattening Frogs For Snakes*	De 7584	
	My Man Jumped Salty On Me	De 7567	A of H AH72
DIXON, Mary	*Black Dog Blues*	Co 14459	
	Fire And Thunder Blues	—	CBS 64043
GIBSON, Cleo	*I've Got Ford Movements in My Hips*	OK 8700	CBS 66232
	Nothing But The Blues	—	Par PMC1177
GLINN, Lillian	*Shreveport Blues*	Co 14519	
	Black Man Blues	Co 14617	
	Atlanta Blues	Co 14421	Font 467214
	All The Week Blues	—	—
	Shake It Down	Co 14315	CBS 66218
GREEN, Lil	*Mr Jackson From Jacksonville*	BB 300733	
	Now What Do You Think	—	
	Blow Top Blues	Vi 20-1957	
HEGAMIN, Lucille	*Aggravatin' Papa*	Cam 270	
	Rampart Street Blues	Cam 494	
	Land Of Cotton	Cam 407	
	Bleeding Heart Blues	Cam 381	
	He May Be Your Man But He Comes to See Me Sometimes		Spi LP1001
	I Don't Want Nobody	Co 3506	
HENDERSON, Edmonia	*Brown Skin Man*	Pm 12095	Riv RLP1044
	Traveling Blues	—	—
	Mama Don't Want a Sweet Man Any More	Pm 12203	
	Dead Man Blues	Vo 1043	Swa JCS33779
	Georgia Grind	—	
HENDERSON, Katherine	*West End Blues*	QRS R7024	Hist ASC 5829-21
HENDERSON, Rosa	*He May Be Your Dog, But He's Wearing My Collar Now*	Vo 14708	Aud AAF-AAK
	Hey Hey and He He I'm Charleston Crazy	Vo 14770	
	Penitentiary Blues	Vo 14995	
	Backwoods Blues	Em 10763	Hist ASC 5829-13
HILL, Bertha 'Chippie'	*Low Land Blues*	OK 8273	
	Kid Man Blues	—	

Artist's name	Title	Original release	Microgroove re-issue
	Lonesome, All Alone and Blue	OK 8339	
	Trouble In Mind	OK 8312	Swa JCS3379
	Georgia Man	—	
	Around The Clock	Cir 1013	
	Black Market Blues	—	
	How Long Blues	Cir 1003	
	Pratt City Blues	OK 8420	CBS 66218
HITE, Mattie	St Joe's Infirmary	Co 14503	
	Texas Twist	—	CBS CL3-33
HOWARD, Rosetta	Rosetta Blues	De 7370	Br 87-521
	If You're a Viper	—	Br 10-354
HUNTER, Alberta	Downhearted Blues	Pm 12005	
	I Got Myself a Working Man		Pres 1052
	Got a Mind To Ramble		—
JOHNSON, Margaret	If I Let You Get Away With It Once, You'll Do It All The Time	OK 8107	Par PMC1177
	E Flat Blues	—	—
	Nobody Knows The Way I Feel This Morning	OK 8162	
	Absent Minded Blues	—	
JONES, Maggie	Dangerous Blues	Co 14070	VJM VLP23
	Suicide Blues	—	
	Good Time Flat Blues	Co 14055	CBS 66232
	North Bound Blues	Co 14092	VJM VLP23
LISTON, Virginia	Rolls Royce Papa	Vo 1032	Hist ASC5829-1
	I'm Gonna Get a Man That's All	—	
MACK, Mary	Stingaree Man	BB 8131	
	I Vouch For My Man	—	
MARTIN, Sara	Brother Ben	OK 8325	Swa JCS33751
	Death Sting Me Blues	QRS R7042	Mil 63806
MCCOY, Viola	Laughin' Cryin' Blues	Ge 5108	
	If Your Good Man Quits You Don't Wear No Black	Br 2591	Hist ASC5829-18
	I Ain't Gonna Marry Ain't Gonna Settle Down	—	—
RAINEY, Gertrude 'Ma'	Counting The Blues	Pm 12238	Riv RLP12-101
	Jelly Bean Blues	—	
	See See Rider	Pm 12252	Riv RLP1001
	Ma and Pa's Poorhouse Blues	Pm 12718	Aud AAM
	Big Feeling Blues	—	
	Cellbound Blues	Pm 12257	Mil MLP2001
	Bo Weavil Blues	Pm 12080	Riv RLP8807
SMITH, Bessie	Downhearted Blues	Co 3844	Co CL855
	Gulf Coast Blues	—	
	Backwater Blues	Co 14195	Co BPG62380
	Hot Spring Blues	Co 14569	
	Kitchen Man	Co 14435	
	In The House Blues	Co 14611	CBS 66218
	You've Got To Get Me Some	Co 14427	Swa JCS3374
	I'm Wild About That Thing	—	—
	Take Me For a Buggy Ride	OK 8949	Co BPG62377
	Gimme a Pigfoot	—	—

Artist's name	Title	Original release	Microgroove re-issue
	Do Your Duty	OK 8945	—
	I'm Down In The Dumps	—	—
	St Louis Blues	Co 14064	—
	You've Been a Good Ole Wagon	Co 14079	—
	Cold In Hand	Co 14064	Co BPG62377
	Careless Love	Co 14083	—
	Nashville Woman Blues	Co 14990	—
	I Ain't Gonna Play No Second Fiddle	—	—
	J. C. Holmes Blues	Co 14095	—
	Me And My Gin	Co 14384	Co BPG62378
	Gin House Blues	Co 14158	—
	Nobody Knows You When You're Down and Out	Co 14451	—
	Cake Walking Babies (From Home)	Co 35673	Co BPG62379
	Baby Doll	Co 14147	—
	Black Mountain Blues	Co 14554	Co BPG62380
SMITH, Clara	I've Got Everything a Good Woman Needs	Co A3943	VJM VLP15
	Every Woman's Blues	—	
	Far Away Blues	Co 13007	VJM VLP16
	I'm Going Back To My Used To Be	Co 13007	—
	War House Mama (Pig Meat Sweetie)	Co 14021	—
	Cold Weather Papa	—	—
	West Indies Blues	Co 14019	—
	Mean Papa Turn Your Key	Co 14022	—
	Nobody Knows The Way I Feel Dis Mornin'	Co 14058	
	It's Tight Like That	Co 14398	CBS 63288
	Shipwrecked Blues	Co 14077	
	Salty Dog	Co 14143	Phi BBE12491
	My Brand New Papa	—	—
	Jelly Look What You Done Done	Co 14319	CBS 64043
	Whip It to a Jelly	Co 14150	CBS 66232
SMITH, Mamie	What Have I Done To Make You Feel This Way?	Vi 20233	RCA RD7840
	That Thing Called Love	OK 4113	
	You Can't Keep a Good Man Down	OK 4113	
	Crazy Blues	OK 4169	RBF RF-3
	It's Right Here For You	—	
	Don't Advertise Your Man	OK 8864	
	Keep a Song In Your Soul	—	
	Golfing Papa	OK 8915	
	Jenny's Ball	—	Par PMC1177
SMITH, Trixie	The World's Jazz Crazy and So Am I	Pm 12262	Riv RLP1000
	Railroad Man Blues	—	
	Freight Train Blues	De 7489	A of H AH72
SPIVEY, Victoria	Brooklyn Bridge		Spi 1001
	Black Belt		Xtra 1022
	Mr Cab		Spi 1001
	Black Limousine		—
	Black Snake Blues	OK 8338	Spi 2001

Artist's name	Title	Original release	Microgroove re-issue
	Organ Grinder Blues	OK 8615	—
SYLVESTER, Hannah	Papa Better Watch Your Step	Maj 1520	
	Gulf Coast Blues	Per 12064	
WALLACE, Sippie	Suitcase Blues	OK 8243	
	Go Down Sunshine	Cir 11014	
	Up the Country Blues		Stor 671.198
WATERS, Ethel	Tell 'em About Me	Pm 12214	
	Backbitin' Mama	Vo 14860	
	Go Back Where You Stayed Last Night	Co 14093	
	Shake That Thing	Co 14166	J.S. LP21
	Bring Me Your Greenbacks	Co 14125	
WELLS, Viola	Bye Bye Baby	Sav 5510	
	My Lucky Day	—	
	See See Rider		Spi LP1009
WILSON, Edith	Frankie	Co 3506	
	Old Time Blues	—	
	Rules and Regulations Signed 'Razor Jim'	Co A3653	
	He May Be Your Man (But He Comes To See Me Sometimes)	—	
	I Don't Want Nobody	Co 3537	

ACCOMPANYING RECORD

MA RAINEY AND THE CLASSIC BLUES SINGERS

SIDE ONE

1. MA RAINEY — *Rough & Tumble Blues*

2. MAMIE SMITH — *Crazy Blues*

3. CLARA SMITH — *Jelly, Jelly Look What You Done Done*

4. MARTHA COPELAND — *Nobody Rocks Me Like My Baby Do*

5. ELIZA BROWN — *Peddlin' Man*

6. MA RAINEY — *Ma Rainey's Black Bottom*

7. SIPPIE WALLACE — *I'm A Mighty Tight Woman*

8. EDITH WILSON — *Rules & Regulations (Signed Razor Jim)*

SIDE TWO

9. LILLIAN GLINN — *Cravin' A Man Blues*

10. BESSIE SMITH — *Hot Springs Blues*

11. BESSIE SMITH — *I've Got What It Takes*

12. MARY DIXON — *Fire And Thunder Blues*

13. LIZA BROWN and ANN JOHNSON — *Let's Get It Straight*

14. SARA MARTIN — *Black Hearse Blues*

15. VICTORIA SPIVEY — *T.B. Blues*

16. IDA COX — *Hard Times Blues*

Index